ANXIETY IN RELATIOI

Overcome Anxiety, Insecurity, Jealousy, and Negative Thinking about Rejection or Abandonment. Silence Your Critical Inner Voice and Enjoy a Deeper Connection

<u>Julia Jacobs</u>

TABLE OF CONTENTS

INTRODUCTION

Anxiety can disrupt every aspect of your life, and generalized anxiety disorder (GAD) can have even more invasive effects. Anxiety frequently drives us to engage in harmful activity. Healthy coping strategies can help you avoid this, but they can be difficult to implement in a crisis.

Various tried-and-true coping methods may aid in times of extreme anxiety:

• Social support - Friends and family can provide much-needed sounding boards and help you feel less anxious.

• Breathing - Deep breathing is a vital skill to learn. It may seem odd, yet correct breathing is commonly overlooked. Using your diaphragm is the proper method to breathe. Your stomach should rise and fall as you breathe in and out. Instead, many people breathe via their chest and shoulders, resulting in short, shallow breathing that can contribute to worry and stress. Anxiety can be reduced by using proper breathing techniques.

• Journaling - Keeping a record of your thoughts and feelings can help you cope with anxiety while also enhancing your physical and mental health. Reduced tension and irritability are two more side effects.

• Progressive relaxation - By contracting and relaxing different muscle groups throughout your body, you can achieve a deeper level of relaxation.

• Mindfulness - Being present and aware of the current moment can help with depression and anxiety. Daily worries, particularly those concerning the future, can be put on hold while you concentrate on the "here and now."

• Distraction - By diverting your focus away from powerful, unpleasant feelings, the strength of the feelings can be reduced. As a result, your anxiety may be lessened, making it easier to manage.

• Self-care - Any exercise that involves vision, hearing, smell, taste, or touch can be done by yourself to boost your mood and reduce anxiety. Solitary nature walks, listening to relaxing music, lighting scented candles, gently savoring a favorite dessert, or taking a luxury bubble bath are just a few examples.

Anxiety in a relationship can appear in a variety of ways. However, the following are the most common:

• Neediness - People in relationships sometimes worry that they are excessively needy. Others may require frequent reassurance that all is well. In a relationship, either can generate considerable stress. Learn techniques to manage your anxiety on your own to build self-sufficiency and confidence that will relieve some of the load on your relationship.

• Suspicion - Suspicion can turn into the fear that your partner doesn't love you, doesn't care as much as you do, or is cheating on you. Anxiety can make paranoia worse. Before leaping to conclusions, remember to look for hard data and follow your instincts. Asking your partner for reassurance regularly might also assist.

• Impulsivity - Anxiety can cause impulsive judgments, damaging behaviors, and hasty conclusions. Intolerable anxiety frequently leads to rash, erroneous behaviors. Breathing and mindfulness exercises might help you slow down and consider things through before you do something you'll regret.

Intimacy is required in romantic partnerships. However, for anyone suffering from anxiety, developing intimacy might be difficult. Regrettably, our Internet culture has both facilitated and exacerbated this issue. Social anxiety sufferers may turn to the Internet as a substitute for healthy socialization. This can foster avoidance behavior by allowing users to avoid being judged and scrutinized in real-life social situations. Avoidance has also been made possible by the use of pharmaceuticals to treat a variety of psychiatric problems.

Relationship anxiety is frequently a self-fulfilling cycle. Anxiety can have long-term consequences and cause serious interpersonal issues. The best approach to avoid these is to calm down before worry takes over.

First and foremost, understand that anxiousness is not a choice. No one is to blame. Second, you should build genuine trust in your relationship. Anxiety is frequently the outcome of mistrust.

Discuss and communicate differences and insecurities. Miscommunication can cause concern and anxiety, which can be alleviated if addressed immediately.

Both couples should establish boundaries. Allow yourself to let go of the minor issues that arise in a relationship. If they aren't addressed as soon as they arise, they may grow into major issues.

A relationship never comes with guarantees. Because you're afraid of losing your partner, your anxiety or worry may persist. However, you can build a sense of peace knowing your partner is with you now, moment by minute, by living in the moment and recognizing that you can't control anyone or anything.

There are 5 phases to dealing with broken relationship anxiety, just like there are five stages to get through any mental anxiety. Understanding what stage you are at and understanding that what you are thinking is just part of a progressive (though agonizing) phase can help you get through your rough period.

The initial phase is denial. This is when you sway yourself (or try to sway yourself) that you're splitting up didn't happen. This also manifests itself as you waiting for your ex to sit down with you at dinner or pick you up at work. There is sometimes no grief in this phase because the realism hasn't sunk in yet, or else you are not coming to terms or even acknowledging your loss.

The next phase is anger. This can be directed towards the world, at God ("Why me?!), at your ex-boyfriend, and yourself. During this phase, you sometimes would like to get even with your ex or act out towards others who try to help you.

Then comes the bargaining phase. This can happen before you split definitively as well. At this time, you try to persuade him or her to come back by making deals or else to beg the person to come back. You may, in addition, be bargaining with God or some superior power in this phase... For example, "If you bring my ex back to me, I pledge I'll go to church every Sunday..." This stage includes an extreme deal of beseeching, hoping, and praying for things to return to the way they were.

The next phase in dealing with broken relationship anxiety is depression. In this phase, you may well feel exceptionally miserable or overcome with desperation, frustration, hostility, feeling pitiful for yourself, and sadness. At this point, any difficult emotions have caught up with you, and they are in hitting you like a brick. You envision an altered future than what you may well be used to considering and feel helpless and insensitive.

Ultimately, and fortunately, you come to the acceptance phase. At this point, you acknowledge the mistakes you could have made and the effects of those mistakes. At this time is where you acknowledge that the person is no longer in your life, or at least will not take part in the same role as they took part in until recently. It's valuable to mention that acceptance is not quitting. You are not quitting in this phase. On the contrary, it is only at the present that you can begin to slowly build your goals for the future and leave your relationship in the past.

Eventually, you will get to the place that you will be grateful for what you have learned in this tough phase. It's also a useful idea to obtain help or have a helpful ally that you can confide infrequently. Remember that you are not isolated by any means and that you will continue to exist, as have thousands of others after dealing with broken relationship anxiety.

Have you been in a relationship where things are going well, and even though you've been hurt in a previous relationship, you've decided to do your best and stay positive in this new relationship because you don't want to screw things up? But then suddenly, out of the blue, thoughts of doubt start to creep into your head... and while you do your best to ignore them, you can't seem to get them out of your head. Before you know it, your thoughts fly away. You start to worry and obsess about the smallest details in your relationship. Plus, you constantly second-guess whether things will work out, and you need constant reassurance from the man you love.

CHAPTER 1: HOW TO HANDLE RELATIONSHIP ANXIETY

You're in a loving relationship with a wonderful person. You've built trust, set limits, and gotten to know each other's communication styles.

Simultaneously, you may find yourself questioning yourself, your partner, and the relationship.

Is everything going to work out? How can you tell if this individual is truly perfect for you? What if they're concealing something sinister?

What if you're simply incapable of maintaining a committed, healthy relationship?

Relationship anxiety is the name for this persistent fretting. It refers to the concern, uneasiness, and doubt that can arise in a relationship, even though everything appears to be going well.

Is it normal?

Yep. Astrid Robertson, a psychotherapist who works with couples on relationship challenges, says, "Relationship anxiety is really frequent."

Some people have relationship anxiety when they first start dating before realizing their partner is equally interested in them. Or they may be unsure if they want to be in a relationship at all.

However, in committed, long-term partnerships, these feelings can also arise.

Relationship anxiety can cause mental pain, a lack of motivation, fatigue or emotional tiredness, stomach discomfort, and other physical issues over time.

Your anxiousness may be unrelated to the connection. However, it can eventually evolve into actions that cause you and your spouse problems and discomfort.

How To Recognize Anxiety In Relationships

Anxiety in relationships can emerge in a variety of ways.

Most people, especially in the early phases of dating and developing a commitment, feel insecure about their relationship at some point. This isn't rare, so you shouldn't be bothered by passing worries or anxieties, especially if they don't have a significant impact on your life.

However, these worrisome thoughts can expand and infiltrate your regular life.

Here are some of the warning signals of relationship anxiety:

Are you unsure if you matter to your partner?

"The most prevalent manifestation of relationship anxiety is the underlying issue of 'Do I matter?' or 'Are you there for me?'" says the author. Robertson clarifies. "This relates to a basic urge to belong, connect, and feel safe in a relationship."

For instance, you might be concerned that:

• they want to be with you because of what you can do for them

• they wouldn't miss you if you weren't around

• they wouldn't offer help or support if something important came up

• they only want to be with you because of what you can do for them

Do you have any doubts about your partner's feelings for you?

You've exchanged "I love you" (or "I like you") messages. They always seem delighted to see you and make thoughtful gestures such as bringing you lunch or going out of their way to welcome you home.

But you can't get rid of the nagging suspicion that "they don't love me."

Perhaps they take a long time to respond to physical affection. Or they don't respond to texts for hours, if not days. You wonder if their feelings have changed when they suddenly seem distant.

Everyone has similar fears from time to time, but they can focus on relationship anxiety.

They seem to want to break up, which makes me nervous.

You can feel cherished, safe, and joyful in a good relationship. It's natural to want to cling to these sentiments and hope that nothing happens to jeopardize your relationship.

However, these ideas might occasionally turn into persistent anxiety about your lover abandoning you.

When you change your behavior to keep their affection, this concern might become a problem.

You might, for example, avoid bringing up matters that are important to you in a relationship, such as regular lateness; disregard when your partner does things that irritate you, such as wearing shoes inside your house; and worry a lot about them getting irritated at you, even though they don't appear furious.

Doubting long-term compatibility

Even when things are going well in your relationship, relationship anxiety can make you wonder if you and your partner are genuinely compatible. You can also wonder if you're truly happy or whether you're just pretending to be.

As a result, you may begin to focus your attention on little distinctions — they like punk music, while you like folk-rock — and exaggerate their significance.

sabotaging the connection

Relationship anxiety might lead to sabotaging behaviors.

Manifestations of sabotage

Picking fights with your partner, pushing them away by saying nothing is wrong. At the same time, you're upset, and testing relationship boundaries, such as eating lunch with an ex without telling your partner, are all examples of things that can destroy a relationship.

You may not do these things on purpose, but the underlying goal is usually to determine how much your partner cares, whether you recognize it or not.

You might believe, for example, that the fact that they are rejecting your efforts to push them away demonstrates that they truly love you.

However, as Robertson points out, it's difficult for your partner to detect this underlying motive.

Reading into their words and actions.

Relationship anxiety can also be indicated by a tendency to overthink your partner's words and behaviors.

Perhaps they prefer not to hold hands. If you decide to live together, they may insist on keeping all of their valuable possessions.

Sure, they could all be indicators of a problem. But it's more likely that they're sweating or smitten with that living room arrangement.

You're missing out on the good times because you're missing out on the good times.

Are you still unsure if you have relationship anxiety?

Consider whether you're spending more time worrying about your relationship than enjoying it by taking a step back.

This could be the case during difficult times. However, if you feel this way frequently, you may be suffering from relationship anxiety.

Calm allows you to try out new soothing exercises.

The award-winning Calm app can help you manage your anxiety. To help you focus and relax, try a guided meditation, a bedtime story, or expert-designed stretches. Begin your risk-free trial today.

What causes it?

Because there isn't a single apparent cause for anxiety, it can take time and devoted self-exploration to figure out what's causing it. You can even have trouble figuring out what's causing the problem on your own.

"There could be a reason for your worry that you aren't aware of," Robertson explains. "However, the underlying causes, no matter how they appear, all reflect a desire for connection."

Some frequent factors that may play a role include:

Experiences in previous relationships

Even if you think you've mostly moved on from the events of the past, they can still have an impact on you.

You may be more prone to relationship anxiety if a previous partner:

• cheated on you

• dumped you abruptly

• lied about their love for you

• deceived you about your relationship's nature

It's common to find it difficult to trust someone again after being harmed, even if your current spouse displays no signs of manipulation or dishonesty.

Certain triggers may bring back memories and feelings of unease and doubt, whether or not you are aware of them.

Low self-esteem

Relationship anxiety and insecurity can be exacerbated by low self-esteem.

According to some older studies, when people have poor self-esteem, they are more prone to doubt their partner's feelings. This is a sort of projection that can occur.

To put it another way, feeling dissatisfied with yourself can make it easier to believe that your partner feels the same way.

When those with greater levels of self-esteem encountered self-doubt, they tended to affirm themselves through their relationships.

Attachment style

The attachment pattern you adopt as a child can have a significant impact on our adult relationships.

You probably formed a secure attachment style if your parent or caregiver responded swiftly to your needs and supplied love and support.

Your attachment style might be less secure if it did not regularly meet your needs or allow you to develop independently.

Insecure attachment types can exacerbate relationship anxiety in a variety of ways:

• Avoidant attachment can lead to concern over the level of commitment you're making or the depth of intimacy you're developing. In contrast, anxious attachment can lead to thoughts of your spouse abandoning you unexpectedly.

Keep in mind that just because you have an insecure attachment type doesn't guarantee you'll always have relationship anxiety.

"You can't entirely change your attachment style, just like you can't change your personality," explains Jason Wheeler, Ph.D. "However, you may make enough adjustments to ensure that an insecure attachment style does not hold you back in life."

A tendency to question

A questioning nature can also exacerbate relationship anxiety.

Before choosing a path, you might want to consider all of the various consequences of a situation. Maybe you're just someone who thinks about everything before making a decision.

If you have a habit of asking yourself many questions about your decisions, even after you've made them, you'll probably question your relationship as well. This isn't always an issue, though. In reality, taking time to consider your decisions, especially big ones, is usually beneficial (like romantic commitment).

It could become an issue if you find yourself in a never-ending loop of self-doubt and questioning that isn't beneficial.

Can you overcome it?

Although it may not appear so at the time, relationship anxiety can be overcome; however, it will require time and effort. And it usually entails more than just being reassured that everything in your relationship is fine.

Robertson says, "I can tell someone their nervousness doesn't necessarily mean there's an underlying problem in the relationship, and they may be well-loved." "However, the fear will certainly linger until they get a sensation that everything is well, that they are truly protected and secure."

She believes that dealing with relationship anxiety early on before it becomes an issue is essential.

These ideas can help you get started:

Maintain your individuality.

As you and your spouse become closer, you may notice that important aspects of your identity, individuality, or even independence begin to alter to create a way for your spouse and the relationship.

As you and your spouse grow closer, this is a common occurrence. While certain changes, such as becoming accustomed to sleeping with the window open, may have little effect on your sense of self, others may.

It doesn't assist either of you if you lose your sense of self in the relationship or change to accommodate what you think your partner wants.

Remember that your partner's motives for wanting to date you are most likely related to who you are. You might start to feel less like yourself if you start pushing down your elements to keep the relationship. Furthermore, your spouse may feel as if they've lost the person with whom they fell in love.

Try being more mindful.

Mindfulness practice entails focusing your awareness on what is happening in the present moment without passing judgment. Instead, you acknowledge and let go of unpleasant ideas as they arise.

This is especially helpful if you're stuck in a negative mental cycle. It can also assist you in prioritizing your daily interactions with your partner.

After all, the relationship may end in a few months or years, but in the meantime, you may respect and enjoy it.

Make an effort to communicate well.

Your relationship concern may have nothing to do with your partner.

However, if something specific is causing you to worry — whether it's them talking on their phone or refusing to see your family for the holidays — try bringing it up in a respectful and non-accusatory manner.

Suggestion

During these interactions, using "I" statements can be extremely beneficial.

Instead of expressing, "You've been so distant recently that I can't stand it," you may say, "I feel like there's been some space between us, and that makes me think you're withdrawing because your sentiments have changed."

Even if you know your partner genuinely loves you and that your anxiety stems from within, involving your partner can be beneficial.

It's OK to discuss your thoughts and feelings openly. Fear may be reduced, but not entirely removed, by their confidence.

Furthermore, being vulnerable and opening yourself might enhance the link you already have.

Don't act on your emotions.

When you're worried about your relationship or spouse, you may seek proof that everything is well.

It's normal to want to feel secure but resist the urge to seek this assurance in unhelpful or dangerous ways.

Keep an eye out for the difference between your normal behavior and impulsive behavior. For example, texting frequently may be natural in your relationship, and maintaining a consistent conversation might help you feel more connected. However, sending many texts in an hour inquiring where your partner is and what they're doing when you know they're out with friends can cause friction.

Try deep breathing, taking a stroll, or making a quick phone call to distract yourself from these desires.

Consult a therapist.

If you're having trouble dealing with relationship anxiety on your own, talking to a therapist may be able to assist. It's also a terrific approach to learn how to deal with relationship anxiety's impacts.

A therapist who specializes in couples therapy can be very beneficial for relationship anxiety.

Assist you in the following ways:

• be aware of your own and each other's sentiments as well as their underlying requirements

• Listen to each other's stories and do not become defensive or judgmental.

It also doesn't have to be a long-term commitment. According to a 2017 study, even a single counseling session can benefit couples experiencing relationship anxiety.

Are You Insecure in Your Relationship? Here's How To Tell

Do you ever feel insecure in a relationship and wonder if your partner is the right person for you? In partnerships, those with a secure attachment style have fewer problems, are generally happier, and better support their partners. Hence, we wondered if you could genuinely train yourself to quit being insecure in your relationship—and if so, how?

Continue reading to learn six symptoms that your relationship may be insecure, as well as Alysha Jeney's expert-approved ideas and tactics for dealing with each issue.

MEET THE EXPERT

Alysha Jeney, MA, LMFT, is the millennial attachment-based relationship therapist who practices in Denver, CO. Jeney is also a relationship specialist and co-founder of Modern Love Box. This subscription box aims to inspire modern relationships.

Where Does Insecurity Originate?

It's worth noting that insecurity goes far beyond trust because it creates a lack of emotional assurance and stability. "You can have all the faith in the world that your partner won't cheat on you, yet you still feel insecure," Jeney adds.

Our core insecurities, according to Jeney, are generally the result of attachment wounds, which is a term used to describe any time a meaningful relationship has broken our trust in the past. "This can lead to defensiveness, which drives others away and prevents us from ever fully letting someone in," she continues.

This is where you start to feel insecure in your relationship and worry if you're with the appropriate person. Jeney explains, "You may be insecure in your relationship and still be with the right person." However, "You might be destroying yourself because you're frightened of letting somebody in too close." This can happen because you're unaware of (or don't know how to deal with) your insecurities, projections, assumptions, attachment style, and actions. If you're feeling insecure, Jeney recommends counseling and self-awareness work to figure out whether it's coming from outside sources or if you're just in an incompatible relationship.

Here are six symptoms that your relationship is insecure—and what you can do about it.

You Don't Trust Easily.

Sign: You tend to distrust everything, to stalk social media sites, to snoop on your relationship, or to feel easily intimidated.

Take action by practicing mindfulness and keeping a journal of your feelings. "Can you question your assumptions and consider a scenario in which you give your spouse the benefit of the doubt?" Jenny asks.

"It helps you fight negative thought patterns and become more aware of where your feelings are coming from," says the author. "Rather of putting your responses and thoughts onto your spouse and then laser concentrating on something potentially trivial and unnecessary," she adds, you'll learn how to better cope with them.

You Struggle With Intimacy

Sign: You have trouble feeling close to someone sexually or emotionally (or both). During intimate situations, you may notice that your guard is raised.

Take Action: You must first comprehend intimacy and what it entails for you and your relationship. Next, consider whether you and your spouse have the same feelings of closeness and intimacy. Then address the source of your defenses: societal expectations, insecurities, prior trauma, and anxieties.

"It will assist you in communicating with your partner so that you are both on the same page." "Be gentle with one another and recognize your differences," Jeney advises.

You Are Easily Panicked Sign: During a disagreement, you are afraid that your partner will abandon you, reject you, or judge you.

Take Action: Think back to the first time you felt this panic and tie it to an event to discover how it's affecting your current circumstance. What was it that you needed to hear back then, and what is it that you need to hear now? If it's the same, repeat that message to yourself whenever you're feeling provoked.

The Why: "It validates and soothes you by giving you permission to feel how you feel," Jeney adds. "It also provides insight into historical patterns and influences, which can assist you in seeing things from a fresh viewpoint, allowing you to de-escalate the panic and communicate more logically."

You Easily Feel Attacked Sign: When your partner asks you to do something, you feel immediately offended, hurt, or shut off. You immediately feel attacked and want to defend yourself by arguing or entirely shutting down.

Take action by asking yourself the following questions:

• "How many of my thoughts are based on assumptions?"

• "Did my partner say something?"

• "Is it possible that I'm internalizing this scenario and transforming it into something it isn't?"

"It helps you confront your thoughts and look at the situation objectively," says the author. "Without the hyper-emotion, you can understand what your partner is trying to communicate," Jeney explains.

You Make Mountains Out of Molehills Sign:

You select disputes and make them into extreme issues.

• You use cruel or definite language.

• You make major disputes over something that isn't all that important when viewed from a distance.

Steps to Take: Consider three to five arguments you've had in the past, and examine them critically. Consider what was under the content you were debating over and look for trends.

"You might be able to detect internal patterns you weren't aware of," says the author. For example, maybe you're sabotaging happiness by making bigger arguments out of minor details because you've never felt a major issue was fully resolved; maybe you struggle with allowing yourself to feel truly close to someone, so you're sabotaging happiness; maybe you have unmet needs in your relationship, but it's easier to fight about the laundry or who they added on Instagram than to address them directly."

You Don't Accept Yourself.

Sign: You have a hard time allowing yourself just to be you; you constantly judge yourself and hold yourself to high standards.

Steps to Take:

1. Work on yourself to avoid falling into a co-dependency trap and never allowing your genuine self to grow.

2. Attend counseling sessions, study books, and put your spiritual or soulful work into practice.

3. Examine how your past has influenced your present and allow yourself to work through it.

4. Above all, show yourself grace and kindness.

"You learn not to rely on others to 'fix or soothe' your perceived troubles in an unhealthy way." You'll gain emotional confidence and empowerment so you can show up as yourself. It also aids in identifying triggers and subconscious effects so that they can be soothed, repaired, or avoided in the future.

CHAPTER 2: NEGATIVE THINKING

Humans have been attempting to stop negative thoughts and remain positive since the dawn of humanity. Without a doubt, negative thinking has such a devastating effect on all parts of our life.

Do you, on the other hand, have any bad ideas in your life? If so, how has it impacted your life? Do you enjoy being with other people while you're in a bad mood? Do you have an impact on those around you because of your negativity? Do you get people coming to you for guidance on new initiatives if you continually have negative ideas in a group? Or do you tend to be assigned monotonous, dull activities simply because you are much more manageable when performing things over which you have little control?

Negative ideas and pessimism can have an inside impact. They can punctuate every element of your existence, stopping you from enjoying the good things. In other words, negative thoughts can make life far more difficult than it needs to be. Steps you can take right now to quit negative thinking and start living a happier, more meaningful life:

Become aware of your thought processes

Negative thinking might become so ingrained in your life that you aren't even aware that all of your ideas are negative.

However, if you understand your thought patterns, you'll be able to replace negative thoughts with good ones more frequently until happy thoughts become second nature to you.

But why is it so crucial to eliminate negative thoughts? That's because negative thinking has an impact on a variety of events in our lives. Poor thinking will only result in negative outcomes.

Stop using negative phrases.

Pay attention to what you say at the beginning of your sentences. When you start a sentence with "I don't" or "I can't," you're automatically limiting your options. Instead, learn to replace negative statements with positive ones and to begin your statements with a positive tone. Focus on terms like "I do" or "I can," and you'll discover that you can accomplish things you never believed imaginable.

Let go of your grudges.

Grudges are useless. Revenge isn't as effective. These are just harmful and can lead to spiritual corruption.

You'll have to break some of your terrible old patterns if you truly want to eliminate negative thinking. Leave the past in the past. Concentrate on the present moment.

As long as you carry grudges, you'll have a hard time letting go of your negative thoughts. As a result, you'll never be able to live your life to the fullest truly. It will be difficult for you, particularly if you have been holding a grudge for a long time. However, if you let go of your grudges, you will be rewarded handsomely.

It's past time for you to stop thinking negatively. Start thinking like a winner and start thinking positively. You will begin to see life in an entirely different light once you turn to positive thinking. Also, keep in mind that negative thinking serves no useful purpose in your life.

The optimist sees the glass half-full, while the pessimist sees it half-empty, as the expression goes.

Positive thinking is just optimism, while negative thinking is pessimism. It's a way of thinking about life, yourself, and certain situations and occurrences.

Negative thinkers perceive the negative in everything, even in the most favorable situations. They concentrate on it, making them considerably less suited to deal with stress, which greatly influences their health.

People who are constantly negative are not always doing so on purpose. Unexpected emergencies, challenges, tensions, and disappointments frequently trigger negative thinking. Negative thinking is a common reaction to life for some people, regardless of circumstances, because they prefer to focus on the small parts of any situation.

A negative thinker, for example, may receive a raise at work and immediately conclude that it is insufficient. Because they are focused on not graduating with honors, a negative thinker who is graduating from college may miss a good opportunity.

Even the most pleasurable moments can be tainted by negative thoughts, such as when a wife's husband cleans the house as a surprise, and all she can think about are the spots he missed.

Negative thinking is a thought process that has become deeply ingrained in mind due to years of repetition, in which one concentrates on the negative rather than the positive.

Kids who grow up in dysfunctional families with critical parents are more likely to adopt this perspective because critical parents tend to focus on everything wrong, making negativity the norm. As a result, even when a child achieves something nice, it is often overlooked. Disregarded.

To assist you in overcoming negative thought patterns, follow these two actions.

STEP 1: NEGATIVE THINKING PATTERNS IDENTIFICATION

"You'll start seeing great outcomes once you replace negative thoughts with positive ones."

A negative personality can be overcome by recognizing negativity and its roots and taking deliberate measures toward becoming a more positive person. Take a look at the following to see if any of them apply to you:

Bad thinkers use filtering to accentuate the negative qualities of a situation while filtering out any good features. A negative thinker, for example, may receive a raise and dwell on the fact that it is insufficient, or a student may receive an A- on a paper and be dissatisfied because it was not an A.

Personalizing: Personalizing is the instinctive reaction of blaming oneself anytime something awful happens. For example, you get rear-ended and blame yourself since you turned onto the bad street, or a buddy cancels a lunch arrangement, and you feel it's because he or she doesn't want to see you.

Catastrophizing: Catastrophizing is one of the more volatile negative thought patterns, and it may be the most destructive to one's health and welfare. It occurs when one reflexively predicts the worst-case scenario in every given circumstance. For instance, if you arrive late for work and know the rest of the day is going to be a mess, or if your child has the flu and you worry that he or she is sicker than you are,

Polarizing: Perfectionists and negative thinkers who only perceive things in terms of good or bad are prone to polarizing. There is never a happy medium. They either see themselves as ideal or as total failures, which has a negative impact on their emotional and mental health, with extremes leading to persistent anxiety and sadness.

STEP 2: IDENTIFYING AND PINPOINTING YOUR OBJECTIVE THOUGHTS

"Try skipping a day if you don't believe every day is a good day."

Recognize negative ideas as the first step in overcoming them. You may believe that you are already aware of your negativity, which is true, but you may not be aware of what is producing it, the extent to which it exists, or how you naturally respond to it.

1. Keep a journal of your negative ideas as they arise. They could be an emotional response to something or simply your ordinary thoughts. You're seeking thoughts that make you angry or dissatisfied. They could include things like blame, guilt, perceived failure, or minor issues that appear to be major. Write down the thought and other pertinent information, such as how it made you feel and why you had it.

2. Figure out where your negative thoughts are coming from. Do you notice any patterns in the ideas you jotted down? Is your negativity mostly a reaction to unexpected events, or is it a result of regular thoughts? Is it in response to someone or something specific, or is it more of a matter of self-confidence? Do you frequently use negative "absolute" phrases like "never," "nothing," "anything," "everyone," and "no one"?

3. Decide on how you will respond to unfavorable thoughts. Do you turn them into disasters? Do you think about them a lot? The way you react can either deepen the negativity you're feeling and make it last longer, or it might cause the negativity to fade away quickly if you keep a good attitude.

These methods can help you become more conscious of your negativity and offer you a starting point for dealing with it. You'll be better prepared to tackle your obstacles once you understand what you're up against." The only way to overcome negative ideas and damaging emotions is to build bigger and more powerful opposing positive emotions."

Have you had to deal with negative people?

So, you finally decided to control your financial future and started an internet business-be it a networking marketing company or your own product/service. If you haven't yet, you will most likely have to deal with these people soon, so how can you prepare yourself?

I doubt there is a way to prepare for this, so be ready to take the criticism. Many times, it's from someone in our family who doesn't understand our business or reasons for doing something different. Generally, it's out of their fear and ignorance that they belittle your decision or say things like "it'll never work." Do these words hurt when they come from someone who is supposed to love you don't, they?

You undoubtedly have a general concept of what a "negative" person is... but there are two categories, in my experience:

The first type is the negative person - they're constantly whining and complaining about everything. They're fairly easy to cope with because if you can't avoid them altogether, you can at least "switch off" when they start one of their rants!

The second type is the INSIDIOUSLY negative person. They don't SEEM to be negative... but somehow, you always feel a little flat, a little down, a little more uptight... a little more negative... after spending time with them.

This second type is much more dangerous. While you can see the Negative person coming - and can take steps to "protect" yourself - the Insidiously Negative person pulls you into their negative vortex before you have a chance to scream!

(Okay, I'm dramatic... but being surrounded by negative people is NOT good for your health!)

You can, however, recognize the Insidiously Negative person once you know what to look for:

-- Their general demeanor (Do they lack enthusiasm? Are they tense or moody? Do they seem as if everything is a big inconvenience?)...

-- What they tend to talk about (Is it always about something bad? Is it always about them?)...

-- What they tend to do (Do they change things they don't like? Do they take action? Or do they "talk" more than they "do"?)...

-- How they see the world (Do they instinctively criticize things, question good news stories, and put down people - especially "successful" people?)

-- How they treat you (Are they critical or patronizing? Do you feel like you have to apologize for something whenever you're with them?)

"Insidious Negatives" may have just one or two of the above qualities (if they had them all, they'd be Obvious Negatives), but it's just enough to bring you down.

Of course, instead of trying to psychoanalyze anyone... you can go with your gut feel:

Do you FEEL WORSE after you spend time with them?

Whether you're dealing with Obvious Negatives or Insidious Negatives, it's probably no surprise that my number one recommendation for dealing with them is to... AVOID THEM!

And please don't tell me you can't because they're "close friends" - people who constantly make you feel bad are NOT your friends.

But... what if you can't physically avoid these people... What if they're neighbors... or family... or work colleagues...?

If you're not careful, negative people can drain you of your life! You will begin to feel negative if you spend even a small period with them.

Try not to change a negative person since it will sap your energy! What is the last time you and your spouse or another individual had a serious disagreement? Remember how much the emotional turmoil affected you?

The greatest method to deal with negativity is to avoid it as much as possible! Here are two key points to remember while dealing with negative people...

1. Keep your distance.

I've had to end relationships several times in my life because of the negativity they carried with them.

Now, I'm not suggesting that you cease loving and caring for the negative people in your life; rather, I'm suggesting that you love and care for them from afar. Stop spending time with them and doing activities with them.

It's time to pick someone else to hang out with if someone in your life is draining your energy due to their negative attitude. Unfortunately, if it's your husband, you'll find it impossible to stay away.

In such a circumstance, some therapy will be necessary. It's strange how when a third party says something to your spouse that you've been trying to say for years, they seem to understand.

2. Get away from it all

Some people believe it is a desirable character characteristic to listen to other people's difficulties. It could be if the person complaining is a decent friend rather than someone who unloads a bunch of rubbish daily just because that's what they're good at.

It's time to locate the door if you hear someone continuing with a nasty attitude. It's like a sickness, and you need to get away from it. Negativity spreads quickly and attempts to latch on to anything it can.

Sometimes, for instance, at a family gathering, you are unable to prevent it. There will always be situations like that where there is nothing you can do but wait.

However, simply being able to recognize the bad will assist you in dealing with it more effectively. Perhaps you should try to be as polite as possible and keep to yourself as much as possible. While the bad is coming out, maybe have a lighthearted conversation with yourself in your head.

Being positive and maintaining that attitude is crucial to your success in life! If you'd rather be successful in your field, you should avoid negative people and situations as much as possible.

Now, I'm not suggesting that you ignore other people's difficulties. If you can assist them, please do so. Learn to recognize when individuals are simply negative. There is no way to help those folks since they do not want to be helped.

Do not allow yourself to be dismissed.

The first step toward motivation is to cultivate a positive mindset that refuses to let you fail. You picture a brighter future, you don't quit, and there's nothing you can't overcome if you have a positive outlook. If you think that sounds like Fantasyland, you're correct. Every day, I live it and breathe it, and you can too. To get you started, let me give you a few pointers.

Pay attention to how you think and speak. The words you use have a lot of power. First, eliminate the term "can't" from your vocabulary and refuse to accept it from others. 'I can't' can indicate one of two things: 'I choose not to' or 'I don't know how to,' so find out which one it is and be straightforward. This is critical from a psychological standpoint since you want to have a "can-do" attitude at all times.

Consider some word substitutions next. In your speech, replace the word 'if' with 'when.' 'If I get this raise, I'll be able to afford a nicer home.' becomes 'When I get this raise, I'll be able to afford a nicer home.' Do you see the distinction? The word 'if' indicates that something might not happen, which is incompatible with your newly energized outlook on life. Substitute the word 'and' with the word 'but.' However, the word 'but' tends to negate everything you've said before it. "I agree with you, but...", for example, is essentially telling someone you don't agree with them. This is cheap and convenient psychology, and we all do it from time to time. Instead, focus on using the word 'and,' and you'll notice that your mindset improves almost immediately because you're instinctively paying more attention to what others have to say!

In a conversation, focus on listening rather than waiting for your chance to talk. Again, we've all done it, and it's more challenging for people who are naturally outgoing and extroverted. Listening is a forgotten art, and being a better listener will make you feel better, not to mention that others will respond to you better.

Finally, right now, ask yourself, "What energy am I giving off to the world?" Be honest with yourself and realize that you have the power to alter your attitude and the energy you emit. Through our facial expressions, body language, and even our thoughts and emotions, we all emit a certain amount of energy. This energy can be positive or negative, and we normally allow it to be influenced by what is going on in our environment. What happens is that the energy we emit attracts energy that is identical to it. That's why those who appear to be "fortunate" are likely emitting positive energy and attracting more of the same. Those who can't seem to get a break are most likely producing bad energy and attracting negative things to themselves. The Universal Law of Attraction is a genuine phenomenon.

Talking in groups with a negative individual is a good idea.

He's in the back row, arms crossed and a tough expression on his face. He'll be picking a fight with you in the front of the room in no time. Oh, we've all been subjected to the plague of the pessimist who is only interested in proving you wrong. Don't even go there, is my simple advice. I've seen too many presenters lose the wonderful ground they've made with their audience because they focus their whole energy on taking on one negative person and trying to turn them around. Remember, not everyone will want to hear what you have to say, and not everyone will be interested in even being in the room.

The person might be negative because what you are saying challenges their beliefs, will cause them extra work, hate change, or negatively view life. You're not an evangelist trying to convert people. You are there to add value for those who are open to listening.

On some occasions when you may feel you need to challenge that negative person. Few tips on how to do that:

1. If you know in advance who the negative people are, try to arrange the room ahead of time to mix them in with the positive people. This will stop the negative people from clustering in the back of the room.

2. At some point in your presentation, ask each person to turn to a partner and do an exercise or answer a question that can only be responded to positively. For example, you could ask them to share two things they've learned, how they will apply these two new things, and why they believe what they've just learned won't work. And then immediately flip it to how they can solve each of the arguments they came up with, so they will work. The main point here is to get them to start a dialogue with another person.

3. Then, have the two partners get together with two other partners to make a group of four. Have them repeat the exercise.

4. Then bring it upfront.

This technique lets the negative person's peers do the work of changing the negative attitude. They may be comfortable the first time they respond negatively to your exercise, but soon they will feel uncomfortable if the other person was positive with what they have learned. Then, when you have them make another group of four, if they get rebuked by this group, by the time you bring the discussion to the front of the room, they will latch onto one of the ideas someone else gave to start turning their attitude around.

If you are a presenter that tends to roam around the audience, you can walk over and stand by the negative person. This often gets them to change their behavior because they become uncomfortable having everyone's eyes on them.

HOW TO ELIMINATE NEGATIVE THINKING

"We wouldn't see things for what they are; we see ourselves in them."

"A good mental attitude entails asking how something can be done rather than declaring it can't."

"It's preferable to be an optimist who is occasionally incorrect than a pessimist who is always correct."

It all starts with a single notion or emotion. Alternatively, you might use a statement spoken by someone else.

Then it starts dragging you down.

As you go around in a funk with your rain cloud above your head, you may find yourself feeling sorry for yourself, frightened, or wondering, "What's the point of taking any action at all?"

Negativity in yourself or the world can rapidly become toxic, preventing you from enjoying the life you desire.

1. Look for the positive in a situation that appears to be unfavorable.

If you've experienced a setback, stumbled, or failed, things may appear dismal, and negative ideas may begin to emerge, threatening to fill your perspective of the issue.

Ask yourself better questions to counteract this.

Questions that will make you feel better while also allowing you to learn and grow.

Questions such as 1. What is one positive aspect of this situation?

2. What is one thing I can do differently next time to improve my better result?

3. Is there anything I can take away from this?

4. In this case, how would my best buddy encourage and assist me?

2. Reminder: what you say and do is unimportant to most people.

When you consider what people could say or think if you do or do not do something, it's easy to fall into negative ideas.

As a result, you deplete your power and risk becoming stuck in analytical paralysis.

Getting caught in your head and thinking that way will pull you further away from your goals and reality.

Because the truth is, people don't have enough time, attention, or energy to think about or discuss what you do.

Their hands and brains are occupied with their children, work, pets, hobbies, and personal fears and concerns (such as what people may think of them).

This awareness and reminder can assist you in breaking free from the mental restraints you may have created, allowing you to begin taking tiny – or larger – steps toward the life you truly desire.

3. Put the notion to the test.

When a negative notion taps me on the shoulder and tries to take root in my mind, one thing I prefer to do is challenge it.

Should I take you seriously, I wonder?

This usually causes me to say, "No, I really shouldn't."

Because I was exhausted at the time, alternatively, you could be hungry. Or I'm overworked, which allows negativity to infiltrate my thoughts.

Or I'm focusing too much on one minor blunder or one unpleasant day rather than focusing on the other 95% of my life that is generally favorable.

This question can sometimes help me recognize that just because I incorrectly performed one minor thing doesn't mean I did poorly overall.

Or that just because something is bad now doesn't guarantee it will continue to be bad in the future. If I choose optimism and tiny moves forward, I won't be disappointed.

Essentially, this inquiry serves as a wake-up call, bringing me back to a more level-headed view.

4. Replace the negative in your environment with positivity.

What you allow into your head in your daily life has a significant impact on you. As a result, start scrutinizing what you let in.

Consider the following question: What are the top three sources of negativity in my life?

People, websites, periodicals, podcasts, music, and so forth are all possibilities.

Then ask yourself, "What can I do this week to spend less time with these three sources?"

If you can't discover a means to achieve it right now for all three of them, start small and focus on one of them.

Then, this week, use the time you've freed up on more good sources and people who are already in your life or who you'd like to discover and possibly become a new part of it.

5. Don't turn molehills into mountains.

To prevent a minor bad idea from growing into a large monster in your mind, face it as soon as possible.

You can also zoom out. Ask yourself a question like Will this be relevant in 5 years? How about five weeks?

This answer will not work in most circumstances, and you were only beginning to construct a mountain out of a molehill.

6. Let it all out and talk about it.

Keeping unpleasant thoughts locked up that are beginning to darken your entire head will not help.

Allow them to leave. Talk to someone close to you about the incident or your feelings.

Simply venting for a few minutes will often help you view things differently.

If not, a discussion about it in which the two of you come up with a more useful perspective and possibly the start of an action plan can be both relieving and refreshing.

7. Remain in and return to this moment.

When you're thinking negatively, you're usually thinking about something that happened recently. Or it could be something that happens. Or both, as your mood and ideas deteriorate.

Instead, throw your complete attention on this instant to snap out of it. Right now, I'm interested in what's going on.

In my experience, if you make it a habit to spend more time in the present moment, you'll have fewer negative thoughts and be more open and helpful.

There are a few things you may do to bring yourself back to being mindful and in the present moment:

Concentrate solely on your breathing.

Right now, take a 1–2-minute break and take a few deeper breaths than usual. Check to see if you're inhaling via your nose and stomach.

During this time, focus completely on the air coming in and out.

Take in everything the earth has to offer in terms of sights and noises.

Take a 1- to 2-minute pause, get out of your head, and focus on what's in front of you right now. There's nothing else.

Pay attention to the people passing by outside your window, the muffled conversations and noises from the street, the smells in the area, and the sun streaming in and warming your skin.

8. Go for a short workout.

When I'm having difficulties thinking myself out of pessimism, I've found that changing my headspace using my body helps great.

So I work out for 20-30 minutes and lift some free weights.

This allows me to let go of my problems and inner stress. It also helps me to refocus and be more productive.

9. Don't let your anxieties hold you back.

One typical error individuals make when it comes to anxieties – and one that I've made many times – is becoming terrified and running away from them rather than examining them more closely.

Of course, it's natural to feel that urge and want to avoid it, but vague worries can become a lot scarier than they need to be.

So, what are your options? This question has helped me: What is the worst that may happen in this situation, realistically?

When you start to ground a fear like that and look at it with your feet firmly planted on the ground, you'll find that the worst that may happen isn't quite as horrible as you think.

It's usually something you can plan for if anything like this happens.

You can also probably start making a list of and taking action on a few items that will lessen the chances of this worst-case scenario occurring.

As a result, you get clarity about the problem and what you can do about it, and the fear tends to diminish.

10. Infuse positivity into the lives of others.

Focusing outwards and on someone else is an easy method to get out of your head and the thoughts swirling around inside it if you become mired in negative thoughts or victim mentality.

You can start to feel better and more positive again by adding positivity to his or her life in some way.

Few things you can do to bring more positivity into someone's life:

1. Be considerate. While driving your automobile, give him a sincere compliment, hold the door open for him, or let him into your lane.

2. Assist others. Give her some sound advice or assist her with relocating or arranging and preparing for the party the next weekend.

3. show up. Listen intently for a few minutes as he vents. Alternatively, talk to him about his challenging circumstance to assist him in finding a way out.

11. Be appreciative of a few things you may take for granted regularly.

It's easy to lose sight of the good things in life when we're down. Especially those that are simply a part of life that we may take for granted far too often.

During such difficult situations, I like to focus my attention on and be grateful for the following:

1. Three consistent meals per day.

2. A warm, dry place to sleep on cold nights and rainy, windy days.

3. I have unlimited access to clean water.

4. Loving and supportive family and friends

12. Set a positive tone for the rest of the day by starting the day with a positive attitude.

Start your day well, and you'll have a good day.

It's difficult to turn things around after a pessimistic start. However, getting off to a good start makes it much simpler to maintain that attitude and happy mindset until bedtime.

Some easy things you can do to set your day off to a good start:

A simple reminder that comes as soon as you open your eyes in the morning.

It could be only one or a few quotes that motivate you. Maybe it's the goal or dream you're most excited about right now.

Take note of it on paper and keep it near your bedside table or on the refrigerator. You can also type it into your phone's lock screen.

CHAPTER 3: UNDERSTANDING FEAR OF ABANDONMENT

Fear of abandonment is a complicated phenomenon resulting from various developmental experiences, such as loss or trauma. This phobia has been investigated from a variety of angles.

Interruptions in the natural development of specific cognitive and emotional skills, issues with previous relationships, and other negative social and life situations are all theories for why people dread abandonment.

The dread of abandonment is undoubtedly one of the most widespread and harmful phobias of all, even though it is not an acknowledged phobia. People who are afraid of being abandoned may exhibit behaviors and mental patterns that harm their relationships.

In the end, inadequate coping with this concern might lead to the fear of abandonment becoming a reality. As a result, this fear might be life-threatening. The first step toward treating abandonment fear is to understand it.

Why It Happens

All of our current relationships' attitudes and actions are regarded as the product of previous fears and acquired beliefs from childhood.

Object Constancy

According to object relations theory, an "object" in one's consciousness is either a person, a portion of a person, or anything that way symbolizes one or the other. Object constancy is the idea that our perception of someone does not change fundamentally while we are not in their actual presence.

This is connected to the developmental psychologist Jean Piaget's concept of "object permanence." Infants learn that objects exist even when they are not directly experienced.

Generally, object constancy emerges before the age of three. Periods of separation prolong as children grow and mature and are frequently initiated by the youngster as he, for example, goes to school or spends the weekend at a friend's house. A child with good object constancy recognizes that time apart does not harm vital relationships.

Traumatic circumstances can cause object constancy to be disrupted. Death and divorce are prominent causes, but even events that appear insignificant to the adults involved can impact the development of this fundamental understanding.

Object constancy can be compromised when parents are in the military, have limited time to spend with their children, or are inattentive.

Archetypes and Mythology

Mythology is rife with tales of lovers who have been abandoned or rejected, mostly women who devote their entire lives to their spouse only to be abandoned when the lover sets out to conquer the world.

According to some psychologists, such as Carl Jung, these myths and stories have become part of our collective unconscious. We have assimilated some motifs and myths to the point where they have become part of our shared worldview.

We all have our myths, which we don't discuss with others but exist deep within our souls. This personal myth, according to Jung, is comprised of our interpretations of the collective unconscious through the lenses of our own experiences.

In this light, the fear of abandonment is linked to these common beliefs, although the strength of the anxiety differs depending on our particular histories.

Prior Experiences

Our adulthoods usually entail huge transitions, such as losing a parent, a friend moving away, a relationship ending, and moving from high school to college to marriage and children. Although most of us adjust to changed circumstances, it's not uncommon to become caught in the process of grieving what was.

If you've ever suffered a sudden and terrible abandonment, like losing someone to violence or disaster, you're more prone to develop this phobia.

Signs of a Fear of Abandonment

Fear is a problem for millions of people. Approximately 10% of persons in the United States suffer from a phobia. Fear of abandonment in relationships can lead to the following behaviors:

• Fail to commit and have had relatively few long-term relationships truly

• Move on swiftly to avoid being too connected to unavailable persons or relationships

- Aim to please

- Engage in unwanted sex

- difficult to please and demanding

- Do you have trouble experiencing emotional intimacy

- Feel insecure and unworthy of love

- Find it difficult to trust people

- Are frequently jealous of everyone you meet

- Have intense feelings of separation anxiety

- Have feelings of general anxiety and depression

- Tend to overthink things and wring your hands

Relationship Effects

The fear of being abandoned is extremely personal. Some people are only concerned about losing their romantic companion. Others are afraid of being abandoned in other relationships.

Here's an example of how a regular relationship might start and progress to better understand how people with a fear of abandonment might handle a relationship. This is especially evident in love relationships, but intimate friendships share many parallels as well.

Getting-to-Know-One-Another

You're relatively safe at this stage. You haven't yet developed an emotional attachment to the other person. So you go about your daily routine while spending time with your selected partner.

The Honeymoon Period

When you decide to commit, you enter this phase. Because you get along so well, you're willing to overlook potential red or yellow flags. You begin to spend a lot of time with the other person, and you always have a good time. You begin to feel safe.

Authentic Relationship

The honeymoon period cannot last indefinitely. Real-life constantly intervenes, no matter how well two individuals get along. People grow sick, develop family issues, start working long hours, worry about money, and require more time to complete tasks.

Although this is a normal and positive phase in a relationship, persons afraid of abandonment may misinterpret it as a sign that the other person is withdrawing. If you're afraid of seeming clingy, you're fighting with yourself and trying hard not to reveal your anxieties.

The Minor

People are made of flesh and blood. They're in a bad mood and have a lot on their thoughts. They should not and cannot be expected to continually think about that individual, even if they care about them.

It's unavoidable that a perceived slight will occur after the honeymoon period has passed. This is frequently expressed as an ignored text message, a missed phone call, or a request for a few days alone.

The Outcome

This is a watershed moment for individuals who are afraid of being abandoned. If you have this anxiety, you are probably persuaded that your partner no longer loves you because of the slight. What happens next is almost entirely controlled by the sufferer's preferred coping strategy and the depth of his or her fear of abandonment.

Some people cope by becoming clingy and demanding, expecting their partner to demonstrate their love by leaping through hoops. Others flee, rejecting their relationships before being rejected themselves. Others believe it is their responsibility to make themselves into the "ideal mate" to prevent the other person from leaving.

In actuality, the snub is most likely not even a snub. , people do things that their spouses don't comprehend at times.

In a healthy relationship, the partner may identify the circumstance for what it is: a normal reaction with little or no bearing on the relationship. Alternatively, they may be irritated by it but address it with a calm dialogue or a brief dispute. In either case, a single perceived slight does not significantly impact the partner's emotions.

The Point of View of a Partner

Your unexpected personality transformation appears to come out of nowhere in the eyes of your partner. Suppose your partner does not have a fear of abandonment. In that case, they are likely to have no understanding of why their once confident, laid-back partner has suddenly become clingy and demanding, smothering them with attention or pulling away completely.

It's difficult to talk or reason someone out of a fear of abandonment, just like it's impossible to talk or reason someone out of a phobia. No matter how hard your sweetheart tries to reassure you, it will never be enough. Your uncontrollable reactions and patterns of behavior may eventually drive your partner away, resulting in the very outcome you fear.

Coping Techniques

If your fear is low and well-controlled, you may be able to manage it simply by learning new behavior skills and becoming more aware of your inclinations. Most people's fear of abandonment, on the other hand, stems from deep-seated concerns that are difficult to resolve on their own.

While alleviating the fear is crucial, it is equally crucial to foster a sense of belonging. Focus on developing a community rather than spending all of your energy and commitment on a single partner. Nobody can solve all of our issues or meet all of our requirements. A strong collection of close friends, on the other hand, can each play a significant part in our lives.

Many people who are afraid of abandonment claim that they never felt like they belonged to a "tribe" or a "pack" as children. They always felt "different" or separated from those around them, for whatever reason.

It is vital to associate yourself with like-minded individuals throughout your life. Make a list of your present passions, hobbies, and goals. Then look for others who share your passions.

While not everyone who shares a common interest will become a close friend, hobbies and ambitions are a great way to create a robust support network. Working on your passions can also help you gain self-assurance and the sense that you can deal with anything life throws at you.

HOW TO OVERCOME ABANDONMENT FEAR: 7 DO'S AND 10 DON'TS

Many people say that desertion confines them behind a barrier they built themselves.

Our relationships are sabotaged not by fear of abandonment but by how we handle them.

Abandonment fear is a basic fear that we can't get rid of. It is a driving force in our relations and is vital and universal to all human beings. It can either sabotage or strengthen our connections.

We can access the therapeutic properties of this primitive fear if we understand how to deal with it.

This fear is triggered when you are attracted to someone. "I'm too resistant insecure for a relationship," I've heard a million times. Many people say that desertion confines them behind a barrier they built themselves. To avoid the agony, they fall into cycles of repeated re-abandonment (abandoholism) or shun relationships altogether (abandophobism). Others are in a relationship but are experiencing constant heartache and insecurity. They're ashamed of themselves for being so needy.

There is a technique to break out from these self-segregating tendencies. First, let's look at what didn't work:

1. Having unreasonable expectations of your partner, such as demanding too much too fast. You overreact and over-need, making you feel less confident in yourself and your relationships.

2. Attempting to suppress emotions. You're aware that your uncertainty is driving your lover away, but you can't seem to find a way to turn down the anxiety.

3. Trying to get your partner to do things that will make you feel safer. This puts more strain on the connection and lowers the mutuality quotient.

4. Attempting to hide your emotional suction cups behind coyness or rage. No matter how you play it, your suction cups are aimed directly towards your partner, and your spouse's sophisticated radar recognizes them.

5. Trying to disguise your anxiety by twisting yourself like a pretzel. You lose your authenticity in the process of attempting to save the relationship.

6. Making your partner feel accountable for your emotional well-being. This creates a dreadful situation where you require them more than they require you. Your desperation grows as the chasm increases, creating a vicious cycle.

7. Self-loathing when you realize your uncertainty is driving your lover away. But don't be alarmed! You can change things around!

WHAT TO DO:

1. Don't be so hard on yourself. The fear of being abandoned is uncontrollable. You have nothing to do with it. It isn't anything you agreed to. It had tracked you down.

2. Recognize that fear is a natural element of being human. Rather than judging yourself as "weak," show yourself unconditional love and compassion.

3. Decide to quit blaming your insecurities on your partner (or anyone else).

4. This is taking full responsibility for your concern rather than relying on your partner to "cure it" (even if he triggered it).

5. Make a promise to utilize your fear of abandonment as a chance to develop emotional self-reliance.

6. Approach your partner with self-assurance based on accountability.

7. This is accomplished not through osmosis but via active participation in abandoning recovery. The tools make it easier for you to take care of your own emotional needs without relying on your partner.

8. Demonstrate the truth that it is only your job to make yourself feel safe. You give up your power when you look to your partner for a solution (and she doesn't comply).

9. Take the emotional self-reliance leap, but be kind to yourself along the way. We might not get it the first time, or we might not get it the second time. The path to emotional self-sufficiency is long, winding, and irregular.

10. If you find yourself asking for comfort from your mate, re-direct! Get your life back on track! Take full responsibility for your well-being.

11. Changing abandonment fear into emotional self-reliance necessitates a profound appreciation of your uniqueness. This allows you to take responsibility for your own emotional needs rather than blaming your partner for your uneasiness. The practical activities are designed to help you gain confidence and boost your love quotient.

CHAPTER 4: THE POISONOUS EFFECT OF JEALOUSY ON YOUR RELATIONSHIP

The majority of us have been through it at some point in our lives. It could be a slight annoyance or a searing sensation inside you that makes you feel like you're going to burst. Jealousy is one of the most damaging emotional reactions a relationship can have, even if it is natural.

Jealousy can range from being annoyed that your husband adores another lady or that your wife is staring at another man to imagining things that aren't there. Jealousy will have a bad impact on your relationship in any case.

What Is Jealousy?

Although most people have experienced jealousy, it is frequently misconstrued with envy. However, envy and jealousy are not the same things. Envy is a feeling of wanting what someone else has while you don't have it. You may be envious of someone's good appearance or their lovely home, for example.

On the other hand, jealousy is the fear of someone attempting to take what is rightfully yours. If your husband befriends an attractive coworker, you may be envious of — and intimidated by — their friendship.

Mild jealousy is an instinctive reaction that causes us to desire to safeguard what we believe is ours. Unlike merely being protective, though, jealous impulses can swiftly escalate into destructive conduct, leading us to act selfishly and controllably. It can even lead us to believe things are happening that aren't, such as mistaking a friendly interaction for an affair or working late to cover a hidden addiction.

Jealousy, whether instinctual or not, is counterproductive. People who have trouble regulating their envious sentiments are often dealing with greater difficulties. Jealousy that is out of control is usually a sign of one or more of the following:

• Fear

• Insecurity

• Low self-esteem

Understanding the source of the behavior can assist you in gaining control over it. Any one of those three factors, or a combination of them, will not only allow jealousy to exhibit itself in harmful conduct but can also cause other issues in a person's life.

What Jealousy Does to Your Relationship?

Jealousy has the potential to destroy a relationship. At best, the envious partner is desperate for reassurance that they are the only one and that no one is trying to replace them. Jealousy can take the form of controlling and distrustful conduct, as well as physical or mental abuse, at its worst.

A jealous partner may try to control their spouse's behaviors by tracking their movements or listening to their calls, messages, or emails. This action establishes a pattern of distrust that is harmful and will eventually lead to a relationship breakup.

The basis of any good and happy relationship is trust and respect. A person suffering from jealousy is unable to trust or respect the person they are with, as well as their limits.

This practice will eventually suffocate whatever feelings of love and affection that previously existed. It'll probably lead to a lot of squabbling and the desire for one spouse to show their loyalty over and over again. This can be taxing and prevent a relationship from developing and solidifying.

How Can You Control It

Jealousy is a difficult emotion to manage. The fundamental issues almost never go away by themselves. Suppose jealousy is a type of abuse that occurs in numerous relationships. In that case, a professional therapist may be needed to help reign it in and provide coping methods for the issues that are causing it.

To go past jealousy in a relationship, you must first establish trust. One partner must have enough faith in the other to know that, no matter what happens, the love and respect they share will keep outside forces from jeopardizing their connection. If one partner is insecure and has a hard time trusting others, this might be challenging.

It can be terrible for both of you to discover that jealousy is a problem in your relationship; whether you are jealous of your partner is jealous. It will take patience, discussion, and a shift in mindset to overcome it. If working jointly to overcome envious sentiments and behaviors isn't working, don't rule out obtaining professional assistance.

Ways to Combat Your Jealousy in Relationships

1. Be understanding of each other's emotions.

If you agree that jealousy is natural, your significant other must be able to do so as well. Someone cursing at you when you ask them to text you quickly if they stay out late is the last thing you need. "You give up part of your freedom when you commit to someone," Leahy explains. "You share some of the responsibility for the other person's feelings."

To be clear, telling a jealous partner, "It's your problem!" or "I haven't done anything!" is one of the worst ways to deal with them.

"Comfort works, and if you think about jealousy as a cry for help, a response may be validation, which is saying, 'I understand where you're coming from.'" You must be open to recommendations on how to help your spouse feel more at ease and then determine whether or not their wishes are realistic. You have every right to expect nothing less in return.

2. Recognize that envy (in moderation) is a healthy sign.

Jealousy does not occur for no reason. It's often about more than your partner like their ex's swimsuit photo. "When you initially start dating someone, you don't have that much to invest or lose," Leahy adds. "As the relationship evolves and you get more involved, you are more prone to experience envy. Because this relationship is important, the spouse is envious."

If you are truly connected to this person, you will experience jealousy, no matter how cool or sensible you try to be. But that's a positive thing since it shows you're invested in the relationship's success. Acknowledging that this is common and then forward is healthier than dwelling on it or denying it ever happened.

3. Make time for jealousy.

There are activities you may take to deal with overpowering jealously toward your partner's attractive coworker or ex-girlfriend (and you know you have nothing to worry about).

"Jealousy time" is an appointment made by the person with their jealous thoughts. "If you get a jealous thought at 10 a.m., you write it down and postpone it till jealousy time."

In essence, you spend 20 intensely self-aware minutes focusing solely on your feelings before moving on. He explains, "By the time you get to jealousy time, you're either no longer upset, or it's the same concept you've had countless times." You can use what Leahy refers to as the "boredom approach to take a step further," which involves repeating a concept, such as "my partner could cheat on me," for 10 minutes until you're tired with it. (Once again, this is only effective if you are secure in your partner's loyalty and your feelings have no genuine basis.)

4. Be realistic in your aspirations.

If you believe it is bad for your partner to be attracted to anyone else, Leahy urges you to examine your underlying beliefs. It is natural to find other individuals attractive, but it is not acceptable to act on that attraction or do anything about it. "The rules that people have can make them more prone to jealousy," Leahy says. If you have highly idealized aspirations for your S.O., you significantly increase your chances of becoming jealous.

5. Examine your poisonous habits.

The actions you think will reassure you (such as questioning your partner, checking their phone, and monitoring their ex on social media) will make you more worried if you don't uncover anything. "These coping methods push away the very person you're trying to connect with," Leahy adds. And, though he admits that sometimes your partner is a liar and you'd never know about the adultery if you didn't read their Facebook communications, you still have to be careful that surveillance doesn't become an actual habit that progressively takes over your life.

6. Recognize that treachery will not destroy you.

"Research suggests that people who are afraid they will have no other options if the relationship ends are considerably more prone to be jealous," Leahy adds. Because codependency makes this relationship, in your view, something that cannot fail, you are more inclined to ponder and obsess over any perceived risks.

Jealousy can help you recognize how important a relationship is to you or alert you to potential red flags. However, it cannot completely prevent your partner from sending flirtatious DMs or cheating on you with a coworker. All you can do is try your best to communicate your concerns and ensure that your envy does not consume you. Everything else is out of your control, but you'll make it.

SIGNS OF JEALOUSY

A person's jealousy can manifest itself in a variety of ways. While some jealous actions are subtle, unnoticeable, or minor, intense jealousy can force someone to act out or damage others. Jealousy can manifest itself in a variety of ways, including:

• Anger directed toward a person or situation that is interfering with something important to you.

• Resentment toward a friend or spouse who is unable to spend time with you.

• Difficulty feeling pleased for a coworker when they got something you desired.

• Difficult-to-explain feelings of aversion for a new person in a loved one's life. A parent, for example, may harbor resentment against his daughter's engagement out of jealousy, even though the relationship she has chosen is healthy.

• Feelings of deep grief or remoteness when thinking about a partner, friend, or loved one.

It is normal to feel envy, but it can be beneficial to receive support when working through intense feelings of jealously, especially if they are rooted in deeper sentiments of self-esteem, trust, or control.

TYPES OF JEALOUSY

Jealousy is a universal emotion shared by people of all civilizations. Jealousy can manifest itself in various ways, as it can occur in a variety of contexts. Jealousy can manifest itself in a variety of ways, including:

• Relationship jealousy: This sort of envy is motivated by the fear of being replaced by someone else in a valuable connection. This group includes an unhappy lady because her spouse is flirting with another woman, a spouse who feels uneasy when his spouse spends time with friends, and a teenager who is unhappy with her sister for going to the movies with her closest friend. Jealousy in friendships is sometimes referred to as spiritual jealousy, while jealousy in love relationships is sometimes referred to as romantic jealousy.

• Jealousy for power and status: This sort of jealousy is common in the workplace because it is typically related to competitiveness. This type of envy may be experienced by a man who resents his coworker for being promoted ahead of him.

• Jealousy that is out of the ordinary: Pathological jealousy, also known as severe jealousy, may be a symptom of an underlying mental health problem, such as schizophrenia, anxiety, or difficulty with control. It is frequently used to characterize jealously that causes a person in a relationship to have unjustified concerns about a partner's loyalty in the relationship, which may lead to aggressive or hazardous behavior toward that spouse.

Mild jealousy is typical in a platonic or romantic relationship, and it is not always deemed unhealthy. It can imply that a person is concerned about the success of their relationship.

On the other hand, jealousy can be harmful if it is frequent, severe, or illogical. A person experiencing intense sexual jealousy may have problems trusting their relationship and may surreptitiously examine their spouse's email and mobile phone or follow them. The relationship may suffer if the partner learns this conduct.

CAUSES OF JEALOUSY

Jealousy can arise for a multitude of causes. Jealousy is frequently the result of communication problems, low self-esteem, loneliness, or, in relationships, uneven interpersonal boundaries. Other common sources of jealousy are:

• Sibling rivalry: When another sibling is perceived to be receiving more affection, attention, or resources from parents or caregivers than themselves, siblings may feel jealousy and envy.

• Insecurity: Envy can develop when one partner in a love or platonic relationship appreciates it but is insecure inside it. People in the job who believe their job is under threat may experience jealousy due to their insecurity.

• Rivalry: If the consequences of losing are significant, fierce competition amongst friends, siblings, or coworkers may result in feelings of envy.

• Perfectionism: People with perfectionistic traits may get envious if they frequently compare themselves to others. While these comparisons might produce envy, jealously can also occur when a person with perfectionism believes that another person's accomplishment may negatively impact their success.

• Trust issues: When people have difficulty trusting others in relationships, they are more likely to feel envious when their friend or partner spends time with other people or alone.

People in polyamorous relationships may experience jealousy, though this is not universal. The fundamental distinction between jealousy in a monogamous relationship and jealousy in a polyamorous relationship is that jealousy in a polyamorous relationship may concern only the persons in that connection. It may also involve persons outside of the partnership, which is how jealousy manifests itself in most monogamous partnerships. Jealousy may be felt by a monogamous couple experimenting with polyamory.

Jealousy has been connected to violence and low self-esteem in adolescents. Adolescents who believe their friendships are under threat from their peers appear to have poorer self-worth and report greater loneliness than those who do not believe their friendships are threatened. According to a Developmental Psychology study, girls appear to be more prone to jealousy than boys. One reason for this could be that, according to the research, girls frequently anticipate more loyalty and empathy from their friends.

You can't have a healthy relationship if you don't have trust. Nonetheless, almost all of us can recall a situation in which our confidence has been betrayed.

But, first and foremost, how do we build trust? Is it possible to re-establish trust once it has been shattered?

This section looks at creating trust in a range of relationships, including helpful hints and exercises.

Bear in mind that scientific research on how to establish trust is limited. There is a lot of study on the value of trust and what it is, but it rarely lays out practical measures for establishing trust.

How to Build Trust: 12 General Tips

1. Keep your word and do what you say you're going to do.

The goal of establishing trust is for others to believe you when you say anything. Maintain in mind, too, that creating trust demands not only keeping your promises but also not making promises you can't keep.

Keeping your word demonstrates to people what you expect from them, and as a result, they will be more likely to treat you with respect, resulting in increased trust.

2. Learn how to communicate with people properly.

Relationships fail for a variety of reasons, one of which is a lack of communication. Being explicit about what you have or have not committed to, as well as what has been agreed upon, is an important part of good communication.

Building trust is fraught with danger. It entails both you and others taking risks to demonstrate their dependability. Effective communication is essential for navigating this. You might find that the messages you planned to send aren't the ones that are received if you don't have them.

3. Remind yourself that building and earning trust takes time.

Building trust takes dedication daily. Make sure you're not expecting too much too soon. Take baby steps and make tiny commitments to begin building trust, and as trust increases, you will feel more comfortable making and accepting larger obligations. Put your trust in others, and they will, in turn, trust you.

4. Take your time making judgments and thinking before acting.

Make just those obligations to which you are willing to agree. Then, have the fortitude to say "no," even if it means disappointing others. When you agree to something and then fail to follow through, everyone loses.

Keep track of your commitments and be clear about what you have on your plate. Building trust with family, friends, and coworkers necessitates being organized. It gives you the power to say yes or no to requests for your time and energy.

5. Appreciate and don't take for granted the relationships you have.

Consistency is frequently associated with trust. People that are there for us continuously in good times and bad tend to have the most faith in us. Regularly demonstrating that you care about someone is a wonderful way to gain their trust.

6. Improve your teamwork skills and be willing to share your ideas.

People are more inclined to appreciate and trust you if you participate actively in a team and contribute. Therefore, it's also critical to demonstrate your readiness to trust others while creating trust in a team.

This is demonstrated through being open and willing to contribute and interact. In other words, listen carefully to what others have to say, demonstrate active listening, respectfully provide your opinions and criticisms, and show that you want to be a part of the team.

7. Always be truthful.

Your trustworthiness will be tarnished if you are discovered telling a falsehood, no matter how tiny.

8. Whenever possible, assist others.

Helping someone else, even if you don't get anything in return, fosters trust. Genuine compassion contributes to the development of trust.

9. Don't keep your emotions hidden.

Being honest about your emotions is a great way to earn someone's trust. Furthermore, people are more likely to trust you if they know you care.

Emotional intelligence contributes to the development of trust. Acknowledging your feelings, learning from them, and acting on what you've learned means you won't deny reality—and that's the key to creating trust.

10. Don't constantly market yourself.

The importance of acknowledgment and gratitude in developing trust and maintaining positive relationships cannot be overstated. Recognizing and recognizing others' contributions demonstrates your leadership and collaborative skills and increases others' faith in you.

People who do not express gratitude for a nice deed, on the other hand, appear selfish. Selfishness is the enemy of trust.

11. Do what you believe is correct at all times.

When you do anything just for the sake of gaining favor, you are abandoning your ideas and ideals. This erodes your faith in yourself, your principles, and your convictions. On the other hand, others will admire your honesty if you always do what you believe is right, even if others disagree.

Surprisingly, you must be willing to anger individuals on occasion when gaining trust. People are wary of people who say whatever they think others want to hear.

12. Accept responsibility for your errors.

People can tell when you're lying when you try to disguise your blunders. Being transparent reveals your vulnerable side, which aids in the development of trust with others.

This is because people see you as more like them—after all, everyone makes errors. If you act as if you never make mistakes, you'll make it harder for others to trust you since you've established an unneeded barrier between you and them. People are unlikely to trust you if all they see is the "perfection" you present.

In a marriage or relationship, how can you build trust with your partner?

Andrea Bonior, a registered clinical psychologist, lecturer, and author, offers the following tips for establishing trust with a spouse or partner. According to Bonior, trust is required for emotional intimacy as well as a good, close connection. Losing trust is significantly easier and faster than gaining it.

Bonior recommends that you "speak what you mean and mean what you say" to build trust in your relationship.

We immediately learn as youngsters to recognize when someone is lying. It could be that someone doesn't keep their promises or that a parent makes threats that aren't followed. Because this method of self-defense evolved to help humans survive, practically everyone can detect the "proverbial boy howling wolf."

As we get older, we refine our expectations and behavior by learning not to trust untrustworthy people, which helps us avoid being disappointed again. As a result, if you're trying to build trust in a relationship, don't say anything you won't do.

It's also crucial to avoid saying things that don't correctly reflect your feelings. Even if they seem minor or insignificant, telling lies regularly will cause the other person to lose trust in what you say.

Another way to foster trust is to become more vulnerable in the relationship as it progresses. When people rely on one another, they feel safe. Thus, we establish trust in our relationships by being vulnerable. Part of this will come naturally over time due to our regular interactions—for example, knowing that our partner will pick us up from work if offered.

It's also necessary to be vulnerable emotionally. Building trust necessitates exposing oneself to the possibility of being damaged. This could include revealing things that make you uncomfortable or exposing features of yourself that you don't find appealing. In other words, trust is built when our partners have the opportunity to disappoint or hurt us but choose not to.

When it comes to trust, respect is crucial. Because a lack of respect weakens trust, our partners' most emotionally durable ways may injure us by belittling us or looking at us with condescension or contempt.

Any connection, even one between a salesperson and a consumer, needs a minimum level of trust and, as a result, respect. However, the more emotionally personal the connection is, the more crucial it is to preserve that basic level of respect.

Unfortunately, we occasionally display our worst characteristics to our spouses. It's possible that we're more likely to lash out at people we know rather than strangers. We lose sight of the idea that respect is much more important to those we love because of the long-term consequences of disrespect.

With your companion, you don't have to be exactly courteous all of the time. Remember, though, that every time you treat your partner in a way that violates a basic level of respect, you are jeopardizing your relationship. It will also make it more difficult for your partner to trust you in the long run.

Additionally, be willing to give your spouse the benefit of the doubt to create trust. Bonior illustrates this point by describing a patient and his doctor, whom he has seen for ten years and whom he trusts and respects.

Bonior defines the difference in how a patient thinks about the opinion of a trusted doctor against the opinion of a doctor they have never seen before. Whereas the patient may be willing to put his trust in the new doctor because of her credentials, he is more likely to feel comfortable with the doctor he has developed a rapport with.

Because of their shared trust and experience, it may even be easier for him to receive poor or unexpected medical news from his regular doctor.

Another technique to strengthen a relationship's trust is to express your emotions practically and useful. A fundamental component of emotional closeness is the ability to talk about one's feelings without shouting, verbally attacking, or shutting down the conversation.

As a result, establish collaborative and respectful means of communicating tough sentiments to create trust. You must allow him or her the opportunity to connect with the "true" you, which includes your emotional complexity, to create trust.

Finally, consider reciprocity while building trust with your spouse or partner in a marriage or relationship. To put it another way, be ready to give as well as receive. Both partners must feel comfortable with their respective levels of giving and receiving.

Rebuilding Trust After Cheating, Affairs, and Infidelity

After been lied to or mistreated, it might take a long time to learn to trust again. As a result, you could feel forced to abandon your friendship with the person who has betrayed your confidence. On the other hand, others may want to keep a relationship going because they don't think their partners' behavior is bad enough to quit it.

In either case, it's critical to re-establish trust after a difficult scenario, whether it's between you and your relationship or between you and prospective partners and friends.

When trust has been damaged, such as after a cheating incident, it's not always a good idea to dismiss all of your suspicions at once. However, if you still want to rebuild trust, you'll have to let go of or suspend some of your doubts to allow your spouse to deliver. But, then, if your spouse doesn't, he or she is the one who is interfering with the trust-building process.

Healthy communication is crucial in any relationship, especially one that has been challenged by infidelity. Each spouse should speak openly, and if a disagreement arises, both parties should "fight fairly" without bringing up old issues.

If you wish to regain trust, keep in mind that your relationship may appear different after adultery, adultery, or other infidelities. It is still possible to build something new, but both partners must collaborate to do so.

After someone cheats, being in the present and moving forward can be tremendously difficult—sometimes, it's simpler to stay in or worry about the past. While the person who has been cheated on has the right to feel hurt, angry, or sad, if he or she cannot move on from those sentiments, the relationship may be doomed.

It is critical, however challenging, to have faith in yourself. The key to any healthy relationship is learning to trust yourself and your feelings and convincing yourself that you will be ok moving forward.

The ability to communicate honestly after a partner has cheated is maybe the most critical facet of regaining trust. Talk to each other and listen to what they have to say. Both partners should consider the needs of the other.

Partners should be open about their requirements and assess whether or not they are willing to accommodate them. If either party believes he or she is unwilling or unable to meet his or her partner's requirements, the pair should seriously evaluate whether or not to continue the relationship.

What if, on the other hand, you were the one who cheated? For example, you may have cheated on your lover, but you and your partner have agreed to attempt to make the relationship work. What steps do you need to take next?

To begin, accept accountability for your actions. Then, accept responsibility for your actions and admit to them. Also, be aware of how your actions have influenced your partner's sentiments. Finally, think about why you decided to cheat and reflect on your actions.

Keep your promises in the future. Follow through on what you claim you're going to do to demonstrate that you can be trusted. If you say you're going to call, for example, make sure you call.

During this period, it's also crucial to give your partner some space. Your partner may need some space to digest what happened, and he or she has every right to be wounded and furious due to your infidelity. So allow him or her to convey his or her sentiments to you.

Rebuilding trust takes time; it cannot be accomplished overnight. Your partner has no legal right to abuse you. Even if you've betrayed their confidence, you still have the right to privacy.

How to Develop Self-Trust

The reality is that you can never rely on another person 100 percent of the time. We do, however, have one person on whom we can rely: ourselves.

Self-trust is a crucial notion since it allows you to safeguard your own needs and safety. Furthermore, it allows you to trust that you will get through difficult situations and treat yourself with love rather than striving for perfection.

Self-confidence is defined as the ability to recognize and articulate one's thoughts and feelings. Honor your emotions and avoid relying on other people's opinions to build self-confidence. This permits you to gain confidence in your abilities to deal with whatever situation happens. Nurturing our inner thoughts helps us gain self-confidence.

Self-trust also entails adhering to your own set of values and ethics, as well as recognizing when to prioritize your own needs. To have self-confidence, you must believe that you are capable of enduring mistakes. Self-confidence also allows you to go after what you want.

People that weaken your self-confidence should be avoided. But, unfortunately, these folks frequently take advantage of you and do not want you to succeed. Although we frequently have no influence over the negative people in our lives as children, we can certainly examine whether or not individuals support us and whether or not we want them in our lives as adults.

Keep your word to yourself. Respect the commitments you make to yourself, whether it's to achieve your goals or to pursue your aspirations. Making and maintaining pledges to oneself is a crucial element of this.

Creating and maintaining a personal boundary is an example of such a commitment. Alternatively, go to bed earlier or see your doctor for a check-up. Developing self-confidence also entails becoming your own greatest friend.

Speak to yourself with kindness. Everyone has a harsh inner critic, which can take on the voice of a parent or instructor from your past who made you feel unworthy. On the other side, the habit of listening to your inner critic may be diminished or removed. Attempt to treat yourself with more kindness.

You can say to yourself, "I'm so silly!" if you make a mistake, for example. "It's all right," reassure yourself instead. It was only a little blunder." When you demonstrate compassion for yourself when you make a mistake, you can better comprehend others when they make mistakes.

Self-confidence isn't about being perfect; it's about believing in your ability to recover from a mistake or failure. Self-trust can be developed by connecting with our emotional well-being and paying attention to any disturbances we notice.

Make a mental note of yourself. "How am I doing?" you might wonder. Rather than disregarding an emotional disturbance, figure out what's going on inside yourself.

To put it another way, be aware of your inner feelings. When we honor our entire selves, regardless of whether or not we approve of particular elements of ourselves, we create self-trust.

CHAPTER 5: RESOLVE CONFLICTS AND SAVE YOUR MARRIAGE

Marriages are rife with squabbles. Do you have any doubts?

Aiming to avoid disagreements in a marriage is a lofty ambition. However, it's a far-fetched notion to imagine that happy marriages run on autopilot, with no marital disputes or disagreements.

Marriage is not a connection in which one partner easily clones the other's set of characteristics. Instead, because it brings together people with their own set of quirks, value systems, deep-seated habits, various backgrounds, priorities, and preferences, marriages are filled with disputes.

However, these marital disagreements must be resolved as soon as possible since studies show that marital disagreements have a devastating effect on overall health and can even lead to serious depression and eating disorders.

According to John Mordecai Gottman, a renowned American psychologist and counselor who has spent four decades studying divorce prediction and marital stability, whether a couple takes a constructive or destructive approach to dispute resolution in their marriage make all the difference.

The good news is that fighting fairly and communicating with your husband are skills you can develop and utilize to resolve marital issues and maintain a healthy relationship.

When it comes to marital disagreements, seize the bull by the horns.

Marriage conflict isn't the problem.

Consider disagreement as an opportunity to isolate the important issues that are interfering with your marriage's harmony. Manage your differences as a team and strive to improve as married partners. Do not expect a marriage problem to be resolved on its own. Take care of it. Stalling is not recommended, and autocorrect is not an option.

You can avoid future disagreements and the extent of harm if you have recently entered the bond of marriage and have yet to discover the post-honeymoon disappointments.

Alternatively, if you and your partner have been fighting to bring happiness and serenity into a conflict-filled marriage, now is the greatest moment to mend the damaged marriage and begin a new chapter in your exciting marital journey.

Common sources of marital strife - These red lights must not be overlooked; they must be addressed.

1. Unreasonable expectations - unmet expectations

Expectations — both met and unfulfilled and sometimes unjustified – are a common source of marital strife.

One partner believes the other is a mind reader and that they have similar expectations. So when things and events don't turn out the way we expected, frustration creeps in quietly.

Partners lash out at their spouses about lifestyle choices, including staycations vs. vacations, budgeting vs. living it up, whining about a lack of gratitude, family expectations, sharing domestic tasks, or even not supporting their job choices in ways anticipated annoyed spouse.

Finding common ground and achieving an agreement is not something that a partnership does automatically. To avoid burning bridges with your spouse, especially in a marriage, it takes experience and a conscious effort. However, you should do it to avoid significant heartburn and a persistent, crippling bitterness in your marriage.

2. Divergent perspectives on the subject of children

A child is a wonderful asset to any household. However, the same children treated as an extension of oneself might become a source of major marital strife. One partner may feel pressured to start a family, while others may choose to wait until they have more money.

Divergent opinions on schooling, budgeting for future education, and choosing a necessary, non-negotiable reproductive expense against what isn't are all challenges parents face.

The decision about what is best for their child involves making tradeoffs to cover the rest of the household.

In addition, to provide the best for your child, a little kindness helps. You claim it's easier said than done in the heat of the debate. But it's worth a chance if you're looking for marital bliss and a safe setting for your child.

3. Inability to manage the finances of a marriage

Issues involving marriage economics, if left unaddressed, can disrupt even the most secure partnerships.

Money problems can cause a marriage to fall apart and ultimately to divorce! According to a survey, 22 percent of divorces are ascribed to marital finances, second only to adultery and incompatibility in terms of a divorce.

Making a full financial disclosure to your partner, going overboard on your wedding day celebrations, and alimony or a child support arrangement from a previous marriage are all big causes of marital strife.

A difference in temperaments, such as one partner being a frugal spender while the other is a big spender, a significant shift in financial priorities and preferences, and a simmering sense of resentment of a working spouse toward the non-working, non-contributive, financially dependent spouse, all contribute to marital conflict.

If you suspect that you and your partner have different financial goals or that your spending patterns are drastically different, keeping a budgeting log ready is the best way to go. As a general rule, don't keep secrets! Like other excellent habits that are difficult to develop but easy to keep, these two behaviors can provide long-term benefits in your marriage and assist you in resolving a disagreement.

4. Time allocation for marriage and personal interests

The reality of married life sets in after the wedding day extravagance and honeymoon pleasure.

In terms of single vs. single-unattached, your 24 hours remain the same (if you exclude sleeping, of course). The difference is how you spend your time in these two situations. And, since your friends and family have dispensed with the uninvited but useful advice that marriage requires work, you now have the difficult chore of nourishing your marriage with your spouse in the best possible way.

Did you say you were exhausted?

KRAs – Key Responsibility Areas – are a part of marriage. But don't let it become a chore in your mind.

Take responsibility for your share of family chores, follow your interests, and urge your spouse to do the same, emphasizing the advantages of engaging in constructive hobbies. Spending exclusive time with your spouse, regardless of the length, is the most devoted way to build an equation with your spouse.

It's not necessary to spend the entire day craning your neck to glance at your phone or looking at each other like a mushball. Instead, keep your phone and other distractions to a minimum. Instead, listen intently to your partner, share amusing anecdotes, and continue sporadic, appropriately scheduled communication over a day.

5.Incompatibility in the bedroom

Misaligned sexual urges, in which you have a stronger desire to have sex more frequently than your partner, can drive a gulf between you and your relationship.

Workplace stress, household duties, low body confidence, intimacy inhibitions, and a lack of open sexual communication are just a few of the real-life issues that can lead to marital strife. However, when you scratch the surface, you'll notice that developing emotional intimacy with your spouse and embracing other forms of intimacy are essential for sexual closeness and bonding.

It is impossible to overstate the value of scheduling sex and going on weekly date evenings. It is beneficial to have an open-ended conversation with your partner. Cuddling up with your mate and discussing your sexual desires, fantasies, and real attempts to satisfy your partner's sexual wants is an excellent way to start creating sexual compatibility with your spouse.

6. Communication breakdown

Do you ever find yourself speaking things you afterward regret and wish you could have avoided? And if you're not the confrontational kind and prefer to leave things alone, you'll discover that this boiling, boiling passive aggression follows you about like a nemesis. Then, finally, it will erupt in an explosive showdown with your husband in your face.

Maintaining silence, opposing your spouse's viewpoints and decisions, passive-aggressive behavior, selecting an incorrect time and location to have the conversation and feeling unsafe in your tone all contribute to marital strife.

When there are so many barriers to free-flowing communication in marriage, how do you resolve a conflict? Approach marriage communication with a problem-solving mindset. Defensively, do not try to make a point. Instead, recognize and accept responsibility for your role in the disagreement. After you've listened carefully to your partner, seek clarification. Setting expectations is an excellent strategy to avoid misunderstandings.

Stonewalling or shutting down is not an option. Instead, take a brief break to collect and process the sequence of events as well as your thoughts. Nonverbal communication indicators might help you cement your relationship with your spouse. Your openness for an open-ended, relationship-friendly discourse is demonstrated by an approving nod and a comfortable body posture.

Finally, it is critical to bring up the absolute non-negotiables in the dialogue. Determine your key deal-breakers for a happy marriage.

7. Personality dynamics that are out of sync and an unbalanced power struggle

Both spouses are equal partners in a marriage. However, this idea is frequently dismissed as a utopian fantasy. Couples with drastically mismatched dynamics, in which one person is a domineering spouse, and the other is a submissive partner, invariably end up collaborating as a caretaker to their spouse, are common. As a result, resentment builds up, and an unjust, unhealthy power struggle ensues, causing a marriage to fall apart.

There is an urgent need for marital counseling in such a skewed spousal equation. A marriage counselor can assist both parties in putting things into perspective. In addition, a marriage therapist can help the subordinate partner appreciate the importance of assertiveness and self-respect.

They will also provide light on the harm that a manipulative or abusive partner does to their hurried partner, whether it is known or not. Following this revelation, the therapist can correct corrective methods to address marriage problems and revitalize the partnership.

Other types of marital conflict

Problems emerging from a marriage's "living apart but together" condition, incompatibility, perceived irreconcilable differences and lost love between couples who grew apart through time account for grounds for marital strife.

However, if the couple has a strong want to be together and puts up an equal amount of effort to do so, the road to dispute resolution in marriage becomes a lot easier to navigate.

A tumultuous marriage does not have to be your reality.

One such shining example is Prince William and Catherine Elizabeth Middleton, Duchess of Cambridge, who met as undergraduates at Scotland's St. Andrews University and made their romance public in 2004. In March 2007, before their final exams at St. Andrews, the two took a sabbatical. The pressure from the media and the pressure to perform well in school took their relationship to a temporarily low point, and they decided to call it quits. Four months later, they reunited, and by April 2011, the royal pair had exchanged wedding vows. Their partnership is a wonderful model for couples who are thinking about getting married. Their disagreements throughout their relationship did not lead to a tumultuous marriage.

Also, keep an eye out for: What Is the Definition of a Relationship Conflict?

Maintain your efforts to maintain your marriage happily.

Even while obtaining a 100% conflict resolution seems like a lofty goal, Dr. Gottman's study reveals that 69 percent of disagreements in a marriage may be successfully managed. Treating your partner as an equal can help couples accept their mutual differences, de-escalate conflict, save their relationship, and come to terms with agreeing to disagree.

When things are tough in a marriage, don't give up just because it's too difficult. You came together in the first place to create a joyful environment for yourself and your partner. Of course, you make mistakes, but you get back up together, hand in hand - that is the core of a great marriage. And you don't just enter a happy marriage; you strive to keep it that way.

Marriage is a start, maintaining a relationship is developing, and working together is a triumph!

When things in your marriage aren't going well, and you're looking for motivation and inspiration to preserve it, read on marriage quotes with your partner to help you construct a happy marriage together.

HOW TO ASSIST YOUR NERVOUS PARTNER — AND YOURSELF

Living with anxiety can be difficult – your thoughts may race, you may dread actions that others find straightforward (such as commuting to work), and your worries may feel unavoidable. However, loving someone who suffers from anxiety can be difficult as well. You may feel helpless or overwhelmed by how your partner's emotions affect your daily life.

If that's the case, you're not alone: Anxiety problems have been linked to marital dissatisfaction in numerous research.

"We commonly find that our patients'... relationships are somehow entangled in their anxiety," says Sandy Capaldi, associate director of the Center for the Treatment and Study of Anxiety at the University of Pennsylvania.

Anxiety can be felt at various degrees and in many different ways — from mild to severe, from generalized anxiety to phobias — and its effects can vary. However, doctors and therapists say there are methods to assist your partner while simultaneously taking care of yourself.

Begin by addressing the symptoms.

Because an anxiety disorder can be tiring, Jeffrey Borenstein, president and CEO of the Brain & Behavior Research Foundation in New York recommends starting by talking with your partner about how anxiety affects daily life, such as sleeplessness. Using the word "stress" instead of clinical labeling can also be beneficial. "Often, folks may feel a little more at ease talking about stress as compared to... anxiety [disorders]," explains Borenstein.

Don't downplay your emotions.

Carolyn Daitch, a certified psychologist and director of the Center for the Treatment of Anxiety Disorders in Farmington Hills, Michigan, states, "Even if the other person's point of view makes no logical sense to you, you should support it." Before you talk about why such things are unreasonable, attempt to understand your partner's fears and anxieties, or at the very least accept that they are genuine to them.

Anxiety does not have a simple cure, but healing someone begins with compassion. "Too many couples, particularly male partners," Daitch says, "want to repair it right away." "You must begin with empathy and understanding. Then, you can move on to logic, but not before the person feels condemned and... misunderstood."

Assist your spouse in seeking therapy — and participate when possible.

If your partner is suffering from anxiety, encourage him or her to get psychotherapy. Borenstein advises that while you can recommend names of therapists or offices, you should not phone the therapist and set up an appointment yourself. You want the person to have some control over their therapy.

Capaldi says she frequently invites a patient's partner to join her in therapy and to supplement the patient's support system at home. "The three of us — patient, spouse, and therapist — are a team, and that team is against the anxiety condition," she explains.

However, do not approach your relationship in the same way that a therapist would. Don't, for example, recommend that your partner attempt medicine or other methods of behavior modification." Allow the professional to provide treatment recommendations "even if you work in the mental health sector, according to Borenstein. "I'm a professional, and I would never [prescribe anything] to a loved one."

According to Capaldi, it can also be beneficial to study whatever type of anxiety your partner is experiencing (the National Alliance on Mental Illness' guide to anxiety disorders is a good place to start). "Many times, people who suffer from anxiety feel misunderstood," she explains. "If the spouse takes the time to do a little research, that can go a long way."

Check out this advice from the Anxiety and Depression Association of America for advice on how to help your spouse choose the correct sort of therapy.

Encourage rather than press.

When your partner has debilitating anxiety, and you don't, your partner's behavior might be frustrating, according to Cory Newman, a professor at the University of Pennsylvania's Perelman School of Medicine. However, you should never belittle or dismiss your partner's anxieties. Comments like "Why aren't you able to do this? What exactly is your issue? "will most likely be ineffective.

Instead, try to persuade your companion to overcome his or her worry. Newman advises, "Positively channel your encouragement." "Say something along the lines of, 'Here's how it will benefit you if you can bear [this] discomfort.'"

Daitch gives the following example of someone terrified of flying: "Begin by saying, 'I completely understand your fear of flying.' Understandably, you'd feel worried. If you experience a panic attack, are afraid of embarrassing yourself, or feel out of control when there's turbulence, you can't get off the plane.' Think about it from their perspective."

Then you might try to encourage your companion to conquer his or her worries gently.

Create a life apart from your partner's anxiety.

To preserve your mental health, create routines and relationships that are solely for you, such as a regular workout regimen or weekly get-togethers with friends. In addition, have your support system in places, such as a best friend or a therapist (or both), in case your partner's fear overwhelms you.

"Whether that means their therapy relationship or just friends, family [and] other interests or hobbies that set them apart from the environment of worry they may be living in," Capaldi says.

Don't let your partner's anxiousness take over your family's life. For example, someone suffering from obsessive-compulsive disorder, which is connected to anxiety disorders, may expect family members to keep everything excessively clean or ordered in arbitrary ways. So, according to Newman, it is critical to limit how much you will structure your household around your partner's anxieties — and not give in to every request or order.

"Try to be respectful while yet setting limitations," he advises.

Assist your partner in remembering that the goal is to manage anxiety, not to eliminate it.

"A lot of people with anxiety problems, appropriately, see anxiety as the adversary," adds Newman. "It isn't. The true foe is avoidance. Anxiety causes [people] to avoid tasks that could lead to a more fulfilling life, such as applying to colleges or going to a cousin's wedding. And this leads to depression."

It may also reduce the number of life experiences you and your partner have in common.

"You could have an anxious life," Newman continues, "but if you do things — if you go to that job interview if you say yes to social invitations if you get in that car and go to the ocean even though... you don't want to travel 10 miles — you're still doing those things." "OK, you may require [medicine] or counseling, but you're still alive."

WHY ARE PEOPLE LOOKING FOR COUPLE STABILITY?

Mention the idea of changing your life, and people react in a couple of different ways. Those who value stability tend to be resistant to change and deny, avoid or abhor change.

For many, stability reflects strength, and change reflects a certain amount of unpredictability, unfamiliarity, and uncertainty. As a result, life looks like an either/or game.

What if it is both? What if what you might see as opposites are two sides of the same coin? What if a change becomes the vehicle to stability?

Outer pressures turn the heat up: Family time is shrinking while family demands are increasing with elder care, for example. With work moving home at night or telework opportunities, the barriers between home and work are blurring. Mobility and connectivity further mean that a conscious decision must be made since it is way too easy to become addicted to instant news and email. The body, mind, and spirit have little time out.

Sometimes predictions of a talent crunch have been made alongside the need for employees to be more engaged and close performance gaps. Regrettably, most of the metaphors describing this phenomenon involve war or sports: the talent war or playing defense. It's fairly straightforward at the core of the issue. People seek meaningful work with the opportunity to grow (not necessarily through career leaps), want to know that they are making a valued and valuable contribution, want to use the talent they don't know they have, want some control over their lives, and seek some hope for the future. The undercurrent of fear from global warming, noticeable changes in the weather patterns, spark in some, an undercurrent of fear for the future is amplified by wars that can not be won and disease that knows no boundary. This negatively impacts health and wellness.

Internal responses reveal coping strategies: Research shows that 75% of employees carry out personal responsibilities while on the job. Mental and stress-related illness is the number one cause of disability. Rates of depression and aggression are on the rise in all ages, negatively impacting productivity at work and home. As a result, healthcare costs are increasing. The necessity of balancing a full private life with work is more significant than money. It is one of the most critical variables in determining why employees stay or leave a company. Substance abuse is increasing along with the various faces of addiction. Information overload creates overwhelm from the printed and spoken word and electro-magnetic interference and emotional sensitivity.

So why do people resist?

Interestingly, addiction, depression, aggression are all ways to block personal growth, yet growth is the very solution to the pressures. Growth means change, and you can not change what you can not see. The pressure hose is forcing change in some aspect of your relationship with you for the benefit of all. Resistance comes from seeing the source of the pressure as solely external.

Personal growth, especially self-actualization, becomes the vehicle to achieve greater stability by strengthening your ability to ride the waves. The question then becomes how to merge these two concepts of change and stability into a deeper understanding of how to lead your life.

It starts with knowing that as you understand and improve your relationship with yourself, you change your relationship with the outer world.

1. Notice when there are cracks in your outer world. Cracks in your outer world mark places where the pressure has built up inside to the point where you have to pay attention. Dissatisfaction and flat feelings are also signals. Rather than avoiding, denying, or resisting, you walk toward the source of the conflict within to see what can be learned.

2. Ask yourself what emotional need have you been ignoring or not facing fully. Face that place of raw truth so you can truly understand what is at the deeper heart of the matter. The combination of traits likely to be found in those who develop cancer, the 'Type C' personality, is described as being extremely cooperative, patient, passive, accepting, and lacking assertiveness. Repression of emotion suppresses the immune system.

3. Observe what strategies you have adopted to cope with the pressures you are experiencing. Understand which ones are supportive and which ones have served their purpose and now must be released. Note any addictive patterns. Addictions mark places where instead of loving yourself, you channel your need into the instant and repetitive gratification that each of the addictive behaviors promises to deliver.

4. Break the pattern of specific habits that no longer help your emotional health. The simplest one imaginable for that 49% of Americans who know they watch too much television is to break the pattern of using the television to substitute for a babysitter, dinner conversation, or something to do. Breaking the pattern means identifying alternate ways to meet your need. The minute you start to see alternatives, you start taking charge and move toward hope.

This experience amounts to gathering information, understanding what it means from all angles, and then applying it to your actions with that newly gained clarity. This naturally alters your energetic frequency, so you attract different experiences. These steps are repetitive. They will surface over and over again and are not dissimilar from washing your hair: shampoo - lather - rinse - repeat.

1. Couples express their sentiments to each other openly.

This encompasses not only love and affection but also rage and irritation. In some cases, stable relationships are not characterized by a lack of disagreement or dissatisfaction.

Even happy couples are human beings who go through the same ups and downs as the rest of us. However, unlike in dysfunctional relationships, all participants in a stable partnership have a strong expression of their feelings. This means they don't withdraw, aren't passive-aggressive or outright violent, and don't repress their feelings.

They communicate their dissatisfaction openly but respectfully and compassionately, and they work together to resolve the problem (not as boxing partners as it usually happens in toxic relationships). And this is true in both directions: not only does a stable relationship encourage the healthy expression of the full spectrum of emotions, but if you start assertively speaking your wants and opinions, the relationship may improve as well.

2. Couples encourage each other's personal development.

When you think of someone in a stable and healthy relationship, you probably imagine being in the company of a fulfilled individual who is a member of a pair and a self-made individual. Unlike in dysfunctional relationships, spouses in stable unions feel safe and confident in their relationships.

As a result, they don't feel threatened when their partner tries new things, moves forward in their work, or picks up a new pastime. When partners are apprehensive about each other and their spouse's devotion, they pour their hearts and souls into trying to keep their partner as near as possible. On the other hand, their partner cannot survive in such an unsupportive setting and frequently becomes an underachiever.

When partners are confident, though, they are more likely to be supportive and excited about their loved one's development and keen to share their own new experiences, which leads to the next shared feature of all stable partnerships.

3. Partners reunite and rediscover each other regularly.

This is accomplished in part through discussing one's hobbies, interests, and newly acquired abilities and experiences. In addition, those in close friendships are constantly rediscovering each other by sharing their inner worlds and discussing how they spend their days.

And, when one partner changes, as it undoubtedly does over time, the other partner is not left out; rather, he or she was present for the process and had the opportunity to adapt. Another approach to reconnect each day is to touch each other in a non-sexual way, which all couples in a long-term relationship do. Hugging, holding hands, and just plain touching and proximity here and there are all examples of this.

Surprisingly, aside from sexual intercourse, which may be ignored or is a necessary component of even the most shaky relationships, it is nearly a rule that when a relationship is irregular, these indications of affection nearly vanish.

4. They are always working on their marriage and love.

It may appear boring to individuals who are used to unpredictable and "interesting" relationships. Still, it is a sign that both couples are emotionally grown enough to form a genuine and healthy commitment. So, how does it feel to work on a relationship?

It entails doing all of the above and being open, reassuring your spouse about your connection, utilizing your social life to provide further support to the relationship, and viewing commitment as a positive thing to accept the obligations that come with it.

Stability in a relationship isn't something that just happens (or doesn't happen). Learning to grow as a pair takes time and work, but it's the most satisfying experience you'll ever have when you do it right.

Meet Each other's needs

Emotional needs exist in everyone.

Consider the most fundamental survival requirements, such as water, air, food, and shelter. Of course, you can stay alive by meeting these physical necessities, but there's more to life than that.

Companionship, affection, security, and gratitude can't be seen or touched, yet they're just as valuable. It's the same with feeling heard or valued.

The strength of your link in a relationship can make a major difference in whether you both have your needs addressed.

Although each relationship is unique, these ten emotional demands are a good place to start when determining whether you and your spouse are receiving what you require from the relationship.

1. Affection

Most couples have different sorts of affection:

• physical touch

• sexual intimacy

• words of affection

• kind gestures

Affection promotes bonding and connection.

Although not everyone expresses affection, in the same way, couples eventually become accustomed to each other's distinct approaches to meeting this desire.

Someone who does not say "I love you" may, for example, express their feelings through their deeds.

You may become concerned if the level of affection in your relationship abruptly shifts. Many relationship problems start from a lack of affection, and it's reasonable to be perplexed as to why a once-affectionate partner has become aloof or averse to contact.

A dialogue is a wonderful place to start if they appear less loving than normal. But, remember, you don't know what's going on unless you ask.

Take a non-aggressive approach:

• "Recently, I've noticed some remoteness. I get lonely when we can't connect through touch. So whether you don't feel up to physical affection right now, I'm wondering if we could connect through words instead."

2. Acknowledgement

Knowing that your partner accepts you can assist you to feel more peaceful in your relationship.

Acceptance, on the other hand, does not just imply that they accept you. It also implies that you feel at ease with their loved ones and that you have a place in their lives.

This sense of belonging may be enhanced if they:

• introduce you to family and friends

• plan activities to do together

• express your future ambitions and goals

• ask for advice when making decisions

You may feel as though you're floating on the outskirts of their lives if you don't feel accepted. But, unfortunately, this isn't a pleasant situation.

Some people are reluctant to open up, and they may have other reasons for excluding you from some aspects of their lives. Nonetheless, feeling as if you don't belong can make it tough to envision yourself in a long-term relationship.

Here's an example of a strategy to consider: Invite them to meet your friends and family if you haven't already. Use this to initiate a discussion about how you'd like to become more active in their lives.

3. Validation

Even the closest of partners don't always agree, and that's fine. But, even if you don't agree, you want to know that they've heard your worries and understand your point of view.

According to a 2016 study, most couples believe it is critical to be on the same page. You may feel misunderstood if your partner entirely disregards your point of view. Conversely, you may feel ignored or mistreated if they completely dismiss your feelings.

It's possible they had a bad day if you normally feel validated, but this happens once or twice. It's never a terrible thing to talk about how you're feeling with someone.

However, if you constantly feel unheard or dismissed, you may develop resentment, so it's better to confront the problem as soon as possible.

• "I haven't felt heard in a long time when I've brought up crucial issues." Could we find a moment when we can both listen without being distracted to have important conversations?"

4. Independence

Partners typically begin sharing interests, activities, and other areas of daily life as a relationship develops. As you get closer, you may notice that you're becoming more of a unit.

But, no matter how powerful your connection develops, maintaining your sense of self is critical. While you may have many interests, you are two distinct individuals with distinct objectives, hobbies, friends, and values – and that is a good thing.

Take a step back to assess the situation if your identity has begun to blend with theirs. This merging of identities can occur organically as you become closer, but it can also occur when you believe you must become more like them for the relationship to flourish.

On the other hand, maintaining separate hobbies might help improve and maintain your relationship by fostering curiosity about one another. Reconnect with pals or rekindle an old interest if you're losing sight of yourself before a relationship.

5. Security

A healthy relationship should feel safe, yet safety might mean different things to different people.

If you're happy in your relationship, you'll usually:

• know they respect your boundaries

• feel safe to share your feelings

- feel physically safe with them

- believe they support your choices

- feel able to share your feelings

Setting firm limits can make you feel more secure:

- "Don't shout at me; otherwise, I won't answer."

Seek professional help if your partner becomes abusive. Physical abuse is often obvious, but emotional abuse can also make you feel afraid, even if you don't understand why.

Balance the polarity

We whip ourselves into a frenzy of action day after day, driven by cultural imperatives and inner promptings.

We are motivated to be overly active by the urgency of what has to be done and the limited time we have to complete it.

This dynamic force eventually runs out, and we become exhausted, depleted, and cranky.

What used to be high-productivity states have devolved into carelessness and error. As a result, parts begin to collapse, much like a machine that has been pushed to its limits.

Our health, our relationships, and our wallets could all be in jeopardy. So, as a result, we go through periods of tension and anxiety.

We may, however, continue to damage ourselves due to our preoccupation with finishing and completing, as well as our myths about never leaving.

All of this terrible disintegration can be readily fixed by just learning to develop the opposite polarity.

What is the opposite polarity? It's a combination of deep relaxation and reflection.

Deep relaxation does not imply more time spent watching television, and introspection does not imply more time spent perusing the internet.

Stretching, wandering in nature, spending time with loved ones, and doing soulful work are all good ways to relax deeply. It's a non-goal-oriented activity. Its goal is to experience being rather than doing. It's a good moment to reflect on the meaning and purpose of your life.

Introspection can take many forms, including writing in a notebook, watching the moon rise above the clouds, and meditating on life lessons learned. But, first, it's locating literature and strategies connected to wholeness.

The season of productivity that follows after you permit yourself to let go for a season will be rich.

We are subjective beings capable of deep experiences, not machines or robots. So while catering to external conditions may help us survive, listening to our feelings and subtle perceptions may help us grow.

Of course, the other extreme of the polarity, where you just spend time within and avoid contact with the outer world, is equally damaging. Then you start to thrive on the inside, but it's always a struggle to stay alive. Finally, you begin to draw a catastrophe to help you get out of your funk.

Recognizing the significance of a balanced life is the first step. Being balanced gives you security and power.

The second stage is to determine which end of the polarity you are on and how you might gently swing to include more of the opposite end. When you strike a balance between action and idleness, everything in your life will fall into place.

There is polarity in our lives, the world, and the universe. Everything has an opposite. This is the rule of existence. The two opposites are an aspect of the same thing; they are not separate or distinct. Think of hot and cold. There is no one place where hot becomes cold; they are just varying gradations of two states blending into one another. Up and down, fast and slow, motion and rest, west and east, north and south, truth and error, belief and disbelief - all of these are examples of two opposing poles or ideas. If we travel west, we eventually reach the east. Going north, we pass the North Pole and head south. Love and hate represent two sides of an emotional scale, moving from intense love to a lessening of love until a dislike turns to an increasing hatred.

Opposites are only different shades of the same thing. The world, our lives, our activities, and our emotions are all polarized.

Poise is Power

The challenge is to find our center between two extremes. "Poise is power" is how this balance is described. I love that statement—poise results from balance. Think of a seesaw as an analogy. Riding this childhood joy provides highs and lows. Many of us seem to find our seesaw lives exciting, but too much energy is required for the ups and downs. Balance is where our power resides; that is the "poise of power."

Walking on a seesaw, we seem to climb until we reach the center to keep the plank level from the highs and lows. Then, one step out of that equilibrium, we go down from a previous up. Moderation should be the goal, even though we often rebel against this concept because it sounds too boring. We tend to quest for edges, not realizing they come with an equal and opposite reaction. Our power is not in the ends but the equilibrium.

Think about how our lives might be different if they were less like a seesaw and calmer while we sit in the middle. Might that eliminate some problems we create in our lives?

Chaos and Order

Another illustration of extremes is chaos versus order. Order isn't necessarily good, and chaos isn't necessarily bad. The trick is to maintain a sense of equilibrium.

What if we realized that in our lives, turmoil is both normal and necessary? What if we recognized that order isn't necessarily a good thing? Would that be useful on occasion?

The heartbeats in a regular or regular pattern. An erratic heartbeat is a sign of impending doom. Without this order, we will perish. The brain, on the other hand, follows a chaotic pattern. The heart, on the other hand, behaves oppositely. Thus, chaos and order coexist in our bodies.

We normally strive to avoid any disruptions in our everyday routine as much as possible. However, it would be awful if something happened in our heads. Can order and chaos coexist in our lives if they can coexist in our bodies?

If we accept that everything is connected, we can let our bodies teach us something about our larger world. Chaos and order in our bodies reflect a larger scale in life. The world mirrors our dichotomy.

Perhaps that awareness can help when we are feeling stressed. Our challenge is to balance the chaos we have with the order we desire. Both are natural; neither can be avoided. This dynamic balance of constantly changing weight and attention from chaos to order and back again can be explained using the bicycle analogy.

It's all about you.

We have a power inside ourselves, not outside of ourselves. We find ourselves in the middle. Not rule over others, but command over ourselves is the control we believe we seek. We gain control of our activities, decisions, and emotions when we attain balance in our life. That is the definition of strength. This is what poise looks like.

Think of all the words that the dictionary uses as synonyms for the word "power," such as "authority," "control," "supremacy," "rule," "command," "clout," "muscle," and "force." How often are these words in the headlines? How often are these words used to describe too many of the ongoing conflicts in the world? Yet all the attention is external. If all is connected, perhaps our attention should also be focused within to find a balance. Could we achieve a greater calm in the world if we understood our internal balance between two extremes? Without internal poise, there is less chance of stability in the world. Everything has an opposite.

Cherish each other like a new couple

When you said your marriage vows, you may have made one promise that you don't know how to keep. Do you know how to cherish your spouse? Discover the meaning of this vow and three ways you can use it to rekindle the spark in your relationship.

Let's Define Your Vow:

Cherish means to hold dear, to treat tenderly, to keep in mind fondly. It is an action word naturally combined with tender emotion in how you hold, treat, and think about your spouse.

Notice how the word spouse sounds dutiful, and it lacks emotion?

You may enrich your emotional connection with your spouse when you treat and think of them as your beloved. Unfortunately, we've stopped using the term beloved today. Yet, it deserves to be revived and used in each modern relationship because it encourages you to see your life partner through loving eyes. This is one way to cherish them.

How Else Do You Cherish Your Beloved?

Embrace A Three-Step Action Plan:

1. Identify the blocks within you that stops you from acting tenderly and thinking fondly of your beloved.

Are you blaming your spouse for your lack of tenderness?

Are you waiting for your spouse to change?

Do you focus on what you are not getting in your relationship?

Have you given up hope that you can revive the spark of love and passion?

Do you expect your beloved to live by your rules, desires, beliefs?

Do your actions and expectations bring out the best in your beloved?

Once you recognize your blocks, are you willing to release them and improve your relationship? If so, move on to Step Two.

2. Change the way you see your relationship to change the way you experience your relationship

It's time to change your perspective on your relationship if you've seen it as all about you and your unmet demands. Now you'll regard your loved one's wants as your own, and you won't be satisfied until those needs are filled.

If this is a new concept, you may need to seek the answer to some new questions.

Do you know what your beloved needs? If not, here are some new questions to ask:

What are your dreams that you'd like to fulfill, and how can I help?

In our relationship, what have I neglected to do or say?

What could I give up to make you feel more loved?

What could I start doing to encourage you to care more about us?

Making our lives more enjoyable and amusing, what can we do to?

Once you've asked your beloved these questions, do you find yourself resisting the answers?

Is it possible for you to let go of your resistance to strengthen your relationship? If so, you're in the right mindset to take Step 3.

3. Spend One Month Fulfilling Your Beloved's Needs And See How This Changes Your Relationship

In the first two steps, you have acknowledged that the success of your relationship depends on what you give more than what you receive; and you have discovered several action steps you can take to improve your intimate connection. Now you will take three of these action steps each day for one month to increase the love, joy, and passionate connection with your beloved.

When you repeat these new actions every day for one month, they become a new habit. Ideally, your beloved also will accept responsibility for finding out your needs and fulfilling them in new ways as a way to cherish you, too.

If you find that taking new actions and building new habits spark up your relationship in the first month, you may continue to cherish each other happily ever after.

Create new memories

I was thinking one morning, as I sipped my second cup of cold coffee, about wedding or marriage vows and how the subconscious mind works.

For most people, unless they have studied metaphysics or mental science or some such discipline, the concept of a subconscious or unconscious mind is vague at best.

Here is what came out of those cold cups of coffee, cold because of all the thinking going on in between sips.

And even though it was 'hot' thinking, I haven't yet learned how to motivate molecules to physically change form: like heating coffee or bending spoons.

Well, anyway, the thought that came to me was the concept of memories.

Why?

Because everything we think, do, or are having to do with memories. Memories that have been encoded into our cells.

Even the way our bodies work is due to memory; most of those functions we inherited from before we were born, all the way back to some universal conception of humans as we evolved. We can call them DNA or genetics, but they're all encoded memories when it comes down to it.

On some level, our experiences are turned into memories that hang around in our personal physical and mental data bank. Every minute we compare what we are hearing, seeing, feeling, etc., with the information in that data bank.

Our subconscious gives us directions on what to do, what to say, what to think, where to go, and how to accomplish it based on what we find that matches or doesn't match our memories. Or, more precisely, what not to do, say, go, or be.

That's what I call default thinking.

If we want our lives to be any different than they are, we must change the energy or vibration of the memories. We must consciously choose or decide on the type of memories we want to store in our data bank. And then go about experiencing them so we can add to the 'frame of reference.'

The idea of choosing to create memories seems a lot easier to me than trying to change our minds or our thinking.

Ask yourself:

"What kind of life do I want to live? What does it look like, how does it feel, how does it taste, and how does it smell?" Then build new experiences to add to your memory bank. When more memories are similar to what you want, that becomes the attractive factor.

I am calling them 'key' memories.

The idea of search, find and show up works much like search engines. Keyword density on your website is a good indicator that the search engines will rank your website higher in search results.

Keep adding key memories. Those key memories have a dominant feeling, shape, color, sound, etc.

Create your vision and then keep adding 'key' memories until you have more matches that support your dreams than ones that resist or even negate them.

Writing wedding vows from the intentional formulation of a vision and dream with strength, passion, and purpose is similar to saving vital memories before they are experienced.

Because your subconscious, or memories, cannot distinguish between what is real and what is imagined.

What will you do if this takes away your vulnerability?

If you've ever watched a romantic comedy, you've probably seen two people who find a way to be together despite the hurdles they face. The explanation is usually the same: they're in love. Off-screen, though, love isn't always enough to keep a relationship going.

The sentiments evoked by romantic love can be so powerful that they can persuade people to continue in unhealthy, unfulfilling, and ultimately miserable relationships, whether they realize it or not. For example, a study that was released in 2015 in

Frontiers in Human Neuroscience discovered that when people looked at images of their romantic partners, dopamine — a neurotransmitter associated with a reward that makes individuals feel good — was released in their brains.

According to Julie Wadley, founder and CEO of Eli Simone, a dating and counseling organization, the way these chemicals make people feel can cause them to overlook rational solutions such as ending an unsatisfying relationship. "People are driven off the medication, the endorphins, when they are in love," she explains. "The chemicals in your body that tell you you love this person are triggering."

While being in love feels great (and is beneficial for your health), these sentiments do not lead to solid, long-term romantic partnerships. Experts describe some of the telltale indicators that it's time to let go:

Your requirements aren't being met.

According to Wadley, each individual has different "requirements" that must be addressed in a relationship. These requirements might be emotional, such as spending quality time with your partner, or useful, such as expecting them to manage money effectively.

According to Wadley, it's critical to communicate when one spouse believes the other isn't meeting the criteria. It's probably time to move on if that person's partner isn't willing to work harder to meet that desire, she says.

According to Wadley, one reason people stay in partnerships that don't suit their requirements is our society's negative opinions about single people. It may seem as if they would never discover something better if they quit the relationship. But, on the other hand, Wadley believes such a mentality wastes time and prolongs a person's unhappiness. "You could be using that time to find someone who can help you," she suggests.

You're looking for those requirements from others.

Who do you want to notify first if you obtain a career promotion or have a family emergency? According to Wadley, the answer to such questions in a fulfilling, healthy relationship should be your spouse.

It's fantastic to have reliable coworkers, but Wadley adds that if you're always seeking help from a "work husband" or "work wife," it could indicate that your partner isn't providing the support you require. "Something may be wrong," if you tell yourself, "I have a choice between talking to my spouse and talking to my guy buddy, the man who is constantly supplying you with the emotional affirmation that I require — I'm going with the friend."

You're afraid to ask your lover for more.

It's natural to be apprehensive about discussing your needs and what you may or may not be getting from your relationship with your spouse. But, on the other hand, Wadley believes that open communication channels are vital for long-term, healthy relations.

"People could worry, 'That'll make me appear needy and emotional,'" Wadley says. So instead of speaking up, people repress their feelings, continue to be dissatisfied, and pretend to be comfortable out of fear of being perceived as a burden.

She says, "Then something happens that breaks the camel's back." And the next dispute may end up being more destructive to your relationship than if you had handled it sooner. According to Wadley, hiding your genuine feelings about how your partner treats you likely prolongs rather than saves the unfulfilling relationship. If you can't get past your fear of confronting your partner, she advises, it's time to get treatment or separate.

Your family and friends aren't supportive of your relationship.

According to Lindsay Chrisler, a dating and relationships coach in New York, you should assess how your close family and friends feel about your relationship. "It's a red sign if no one in the community supports your relationship," she says. Also, according to Chrisler, it's a good idea to listen to the thoughts of those who love and support you if the person you're in love with isn't making you happy.

If you choose to ignore your friends and family's concerns, you could notice another clue that it's time to stop the relationship: "You're starting to lie to your friends, you're starting to lie to yourself," Chrisler says. When you avoid listening to your loved ones' concerns by isolating yourself from them, they're usually right - the connection isn't working, she adds.

You believe you owe it to your spouse to stay with him or her.

According to a 2016 study published in Current Psychology, people are more inclined to continue in relationships in which they have already committed time and effort. This is related to the "sunk cost effect," financial investing phenomena. Even if the decision does not make you happy, a previous investment leads to a continual investment.

"Time does not always equal success when it comes to people and relationships," says Wadley, who adds that many of her clients are hesitant to leave an unhappy relationship because they want to reap the benefits of their investment.

However, merely devoting extra time to a relationship with someone you care about will not solve the issues. If neither partner is prepared to meet the other's wants, the relationship is unlikely to last much longer.

For more than a year, you've been working on your relationship.

According to Chrisler, there is a higher incentive to work through issues when two people are madly in love and have been together for years or have created a family together. She encourages couples counseling if both sides want the relationship to work. She does, however, recommend that you set a one-year time limit.

"If you spend too much time indecisiveness, the foundation of your relationship will deteriorate to the point where you won't be able to repair it," she warns.

According to Chrisler, after about a year of deliberately working on the relationship and failing to meet each other's requirements, the difficult decision to break up is generally the best solution.

You don't get along with your partner.

Chrisler claims that you can be in love with someone you don't like, which may seem paradoxical. If that's the case, you might get by day to day, but getting through terrible times together will be practically impossible.

People in good, loving relationships maintain the perspective that "this is my friend, and I'm going to get through this with this person," according to Chrisler. But, "I'm not sure how you get through those things without liking them," she adds.

Even when a relationship isn't working, Chrisler says it's never easy to walk away from someone you care about. She claims that the secret is to listen to your logical brain rather than the euphoric physiological response that love might cause.

Your partner is abusive.

It is possible to love an abusive partner in an abusive relationship. According to a 2015 poll by the Centers for Disease Control and Prevention, one in four women and one in ten males have been victims of intimate partner abuse. According to a 2010 research by the National Institute of Mental Health, more than half of the women polled thought their abusive husbands were "very dependable." One-fifth of the women polled felt the guys had substantial favorable characteristics, such as "being affectionate." Researchers discovered that these beliefs influenced some victims' decisions to stay in abusive relationships for various reasons, including isolation, extortion, and physical abuse.

Chrisler thinks it's critical to find a safe path out when it comes to any form of abuse. "Getting out of those connections is difficult," she explains. "You have to love yourself completely."

HOW OBSESSIVE ATTACHMENT IMPACTS COUPLES

Our attachment pattern influences everything from our partner selection to how successfully our relationships grow to, regrettably, how they end. As a result, recognizing our attachment pattern might help us comprehend our relationship's strengths and weaknesses. Moreover, early childhood attachments build an attachment pattern that serves as a functioning model for adult partnerships.

This attachment model impacts how we respond to our wants and how we go about meeting them. Individuals with a stable attachment pattern can effortlessly connect with others, addressing their own and others' needs. Conversely, when a person has an anxious or avoidant attachment pattern and chooses a mate who fits that maladaptive pattern, he or she is more than likely choosing someone who will not make him or her happy.

A person with a functioning model of anxious/preoccupied attachment, for example, believes that to grow close to someone and have their needs filled, they must be with them all of the time and receive reassurance. Therefore, they chose someone lonely and difficult to connect with to sustain this picture of reality. On the other hand, people who have a dismissive/avoidant attachment model tend to be aloof because they believe that the best way to get your needs satisfied is to pretend you don't have any. Then he or she chooses someone who is possessive or excessively demanding of attention.

In some ways, partnering with individuals who support our assumptions sets us up for failure. For example, if we grew up with an insecure attachment pattern, we may project or want to reproduce similar patterns of interacting as adults, even if these patterns injure us and are not in our best interests.

There are four different types of attachments.

Dr. Phillip Shaver and Dr. Cindy Hazan discovered that roughly 60% of persons have a secure attachment, 20% have an avoidant attachment, and 20% have an anxious attachment in their study. So, what exactly does this imply? First, you may ask yourself some questions to figure out your attachment type and how it affects your relationships. Next, Dr. Phillip Shaver and I will offer a CE Webinar on "Secure and Insecure Love: An Attachment Perspective" on August 13. Then, you can start identifying your attachment type by studying the four adult attachment types and how they often affect couples' relationships.

Secure attachment – Adults who are securely bonded are more fulfilled in their relationships. The better a child gets to know his parents, the greater his feeling of security. A comfortable adult has a similar relationship with their love partner, feeling safe and bonded yet still allowing them and their spouse to move around freely.

When a secure adult's partner is distressed, they offer support. They also seek comfort from their companion when they are distressed. Their relationship is open, honest, and equal, with both persons feeling independent but still loving one other. Securely bonded couples are less likely to engage in what my father, psychologist Robert Firestone, calls a "Fantasy Bond," an imaginary connection that provides a sense of security. A couple foregoes actual acts of love in a fantasy relationship favoring more routine, emotionally cut-off interactions.

Attachment to an Anxious Preoccupied Person – People with an uneasy attachment, unlike partners securely attached, are trying to develop a dream link. They frequently experience emotional hunger instead of genuine love or trust for their relationship. They rely on their partner to save or complete them regularly. They cling to their relationship for a sense of protection and security, but they take activities that push their relationship away.

Even if anxiously attached people appear desperate or insecure, their actions frequently compound their worries. For example, they become clinging, demanding, or possessive toward their partner when they are unclear of their spouse's feelings and feel unsafe in their relationship. They may also view their partner's independent behavior as confirmation of their anxieties.

If their partner, for example, begins to socialize more with friends, they may believe to themselves, "See? He isn't truly in love with me. This indicates that he intends to abandon me. Dismissive-Avoidant Attachment — People who have a dismissive-avoidant attachment tend to emotionally remove themselves from their partner. They may seek isolation and feel "pseudo-independent," assuming parental responsibilities.

As a result, they often come across as self-centered and overly concerned with their creature comforts.

Pseudo-independence is a figment of the imagination because every human being needs connection. People with a dismissive-avoidant attachment, on the other hand, tend to live more reflective lives, dismissing the importance of loved ones and readily separating from them. They are frequently mentally protected and can emotionally shut down. They may switch off their feelings and not react even in highly charged or emotional situations. For instance, if their spouse is upset and threatens to leave them, they can answer with, "I don't care."

Fearful-Avoidant Attachment — A person with a terrified-avoidant attachment lives in a state of ambivalence, fearful of being both too near to and too far away from people. They make every effort to suppress their emotions, but they are unable to do so. They can't simply ignore their anxiousness or deny their feelings. Instead, their feelings overwhelm them, and they frequently suffer emotional storms. Their moods are often contradictory or unpredictable. They view their relationships through the lens of the working model, which states that you must go toward people to have your needs filled, but that if you get too near to others, they will hurt you. To put it another way, the person they want to go to for safety is also the one they are afraid to be near. As a result, they lack a well-thought-out strategy for ensuring that others address their demands.

As adults, these people are more likely to be in turbulent or dramatic relationships with many highs and lows. They are generally afraid of being abandoned, yet they often struggle with intimacy. When they feel rejected, they may cling to their spouse, but when they are close, they may feel confined. The timing between them and their companion often appears to be incorrect. A person who suffers from fearful-avoidant attachment is more likely to be in an abusive relationship.

The attachment style you acquired as a child due to your bond with a parent or early caretaker does not determine your adult relationships. Instead, you can find ways you're guarding yourself against getting close and being emotionally engaged if you learn about your attachment type and work toward building an "earned secure attachment."

Choose a partner with a secure attachment style and work on growing yourself in that relationship to test your defenses. Therapy can also assist in the modification of dysfunctional attachment patterns. Both you and your partner can fight the doubts and worries reinforced by your age-old functioning models by becoming conscious of your attachment style and developing new attachment styles for a meaningful, loving connection.

CHAPTER 6: INSECURITY IN RELATIONSHIP

Is it feasible to end up in divorce court as a result of relationship insecurity? I believe it depends on the individual, but insecurity in partnerships can either confirm suspicions or lead a partner to leave due to the madness typically linked with insecurity.

Some folks are so insecure that they have a hard time relating to their spouse or others. As a result, some can have a difficult time adjusting to the married life. Sure, the relationship may have been wonderful before the marriage, but insecurity in relationships can creep in once the wedding takes place and commitments are made.

There may be some past relationships where a person has been hurt, causing insecurity in the marriage. Perhaps lingering memories of a difficult breakup in the past are feeling insecure feelings in the marriage. There may have been infidelity or even an ugly divorce in a previous relationship that's driving the insecurity.

You may find yourself or others who are insecure always trying to answer the "what if" questions;

• What if I'm not able to meet all of his/her needs and expectations?

• What if he/she finds someone else better than me?

• What if my appearance changes? Will he or she lose interest in me?

Sometimes it's a struggle for folks to believe that they are good enough for their spouse.

So with anxiety and fear constantly on their mind, their behavior becomes troublesome and puts stress on the marriage.

Some people are obsessed with making sure their partner is content and approves of their connection. The insecure person may closely examine every word, facial expression, or act by their spouse and worry unnecessarily. Always wondering "is he/she unhappy with me"; or "why is he/she not smiling as much anymore" or "he/she must be leaving me because we haven't been intimate in 2 weeks".

The problem with insecurity in relationships is that sometimes it's hard to see real issues that may need addressing because of the over-reaction to everything.

Here are some things you may do to improve your marriage if you or your partner is dealing with insecurity in your relationship:

1. Stop trying to be a mind reader. Since you know there is a level of insecurity, talk it out and create a safe environment for asking the question. Instead of looking at something your spouse did or didn't do and wondering "what if," ask him or her for the sake of clarity why or what exactly was meant or done. Don't rely on your creativity to solve the problem.

2. Avoid comparing your marriage to others or perhaps past relationships. If you keep focusing on broken or failed relationships, you will drive your current marriage there as well.

3. Don't try to change your spouse to make you more secure. Instead, you should strengthen your relationship so that your insecurity doesn't cause you to control every word, action, or place your spouse goes.

Insecurity in relationships can result in either the insecure person sabotaging the marriage out of fear and anxiety or simply creating a frustrating unhappy marriage.

Relationship insecurity is a terrible thing to have to live with. Whether it's you or your partner, insecurity can take various forms that you may not even notice. Sometimes we question ourselves and cannot achieve anything, or we believe that the people we care about don't care about us. That is a sign of insecurity.

Men and women experience insecurity. Insecurity is when we lack confidence in our self-worth or don't trust ourselves to do something and accomplish it. We don't even realize sometimes when we are showing signs of insecurity or when someone else is.

Those signs are shyness, paranoia, or being withdrawn socially. In turn, we start becoming arrogant to mask our feelings, and we become aggressive. We also isolate ourselves from people and do not even realize it. Focusing all our time on something that takes us away from our loved ones is a sign of insecurity.

Insecurity can also make your partner feel like they have to say things that lift and motivate you constantly. This causes exhaustion and hopelessness for your partner. You make them think that you'll never come out of this depression, and this could make them give up.

When we ignore our partners in relationships, this is also a sign of insecurity. Even if we aren't aware of it, refusing to spend is a type of insecurity. You have to realize that everything your partner says and does is not a direct attack against you. To save a relationship from insecurity, you have to have communication.

You have to start talking about what's on your mind to your partner. Start self-reflecting and recognizing your value and self-worth, and seeing how you can accomplish things you set your mind to and depend on to do something.

Start recognizing when you feel insecure. For example, when you feel jealous, mistrust, not open up and talk, or put yourself down. Instead, discuss with your partner what is causing you to feel this way. Take this seriously because people have hurt themselves physically and mentally over insecurity.

You have to start talking and opening up, no matter how difficult or scared you may be to do so. The only way to beat insecurity in relationships is to communicate.

Lots of people experience insecurity in their relationships from time to time. Relationships can be quite fragile things, so it's not uncommon for worries and fears to crop up in them. Here are some ideas to help you to overcome insecurity in relationships.

Talk about your feelings.

There's a good chance that if you've got worries, so has your partner. If they're open to it, talking about your feelings can help a great deal. If you don't think you can discuss your feelings with your partner, pick a close friend. This will have the advantage that they probably know both of you and can help you see the other side's perspective.

Learn to relax

Sometimes insecurities are just a manifestation of other things that are happening in your life. If you take the time out to relax - ideally with your partner - then you may well find that the feelings of insecurity start to reduce.

Don't overanalyze

Sometimes, something you pick up as "they don't like me as much anymore" is your partner having a bad day themselves. It's unlikely that you know everything going on in their life, and it could be that you're just the nearest place to vent their worries.

Learn to trust

Quite often, insecurity develops because there's something in your relationship that you don't trust. For example, is the working that late that often? That kind of question can lead to a major bout of insecurity that festers away inside you, eventually causing you to break up the relationship even though nothing was happening in the first place.

Stop feeling so jealous.

Insecurity in relationships often rears its ugly head in the form of jealousy. Of course, it's easy to say "stop feeling jealous," but we both know it's more complicated than that. So again, discussing it with a friend or even a professional counselor can be a helpful approach to determine whether the jealousy is justified and how to overcome the sentiments.

Getting rid of your feelings of insecurity probably won't happen overnight, but if you can find ways to chip away at the feelings, you'll find that they probably crop up less often, and when they do, they're less intense. Spend some time working on the reasons that you experience insecurity. Tackle the smaller ones first - the issues that you try to shrug off but are still eating away at you.

Love probably doesn't hurt. Insecurity in relationships, however, is excruciating. You are continually concerned that you may be abandoned or that your sweetheart will seek love elsewhere.

Top suggestions for overcoming relationship uncertainty and regaining your peace of mind:

1. Begin to place a higher value on yourself. This may not appear to be an option at first, but you must recognize that your insecurity in relationships arises from self-doubt. "What makes him or her desire to be with me...?"("when they could be with someone so much better" being the subtext)? This is the question underlying your feelings of insecurity. Focus on your talents, strengths, and, yes, your physical beauty too, and you will discover your insecurity in relationships beginning to subside.

Not only that, but by default, you'll become more desirable because people who genuinely feel good "in their own skin" are attractive and good to be around.

2. Ask yourself if it's true. For heavens' sake, don't ask your lover this! But do ask yourself. If there's no way to be sure, then it is equally true to say (to yourself) that it is not happening! Why torture yourself with made-up horror stories and worsen your nervousness in relationships when you discover that you're just telling yourself an unjustified falsehood that's making everyone's life uncomfortable?

To fully understand my point here, re-read tip number one! Unless you have good reason to think it is true, you create your self-torture - and that doesn't make sense. It is just your own voracious need for reassurance - which will drive anyone away in the end! You can't keep someone close by exhibiting your insecurity in relationships like a wound. That doesn't attract love anyway. It might attract sympathy for a while, but that's no basis for a relationship!

3. Get over it - it happens! This may appear to be an odd concept for reducing your uneasiness in relationships to the size of a pinhead, but where did you learn that relationships work according to the laws in your head? It doesn't mean that it's okay for anyone to behave in this way or treat you in such a way - I'm not saying that at all. I'm saying I don't take it personally! That relationship wasn't right for you, that's all. Have you ever been disappointed that a restaurant you thought was going to serve delicious food came up with a very average menu? The restaurant owner didn't do that especially for you - but you know you won't eat there again. It isn't about you!

The same principle is true for relationships - and your insecurity in relationships. Once you get that the other person has his or her issues, then you can tell yourself that they missed a great opportunity to spend time with you - and walk away.

Your dignity is intact, your ego is far less bruised, and you'll have no need to carry any sense of insecurity in relationships into the next encounter.

Love is just one of life's greatest adventures, that's all! So live it, love it, and move on if you have to. But whatever you do, don't let insecurity in relationships keep you from it!

WHAT ARE THE INSECURITY SYMPTOMS, AND HOW DO YOU IDENTIFY THEM?

We can't always account for every unknown variable in a relationship, so when there's trouble, insecurity in relationships appear. Whether it's on his side or her side, the symptoms are relatively the same. At first, it may be hard to accept and may even deny the problem in the relationship, but that's the last thing you want to do. Below are three signs you should be aware of and act on as soon as possible.

Being Too Defensive

For men, this may be the least present sign of insecurity in a relationship. Being overly sensitive to what she says can be negative in your relationship. If you can't take a joke or criticism, you can be sure the relationship isn't going to last very long. If pride or ego is what's keeping you, throw it away. You'll find your partner is much likely to appreciate you more if you can be a man about these sorts of things.

Being Irrationally Jealous

Checking up on her and calling her every five minutes is just about the same as stalking her. She doesn't like it, you're only exhausting yourself, and she'll probably get a restraining order at some point. A lack of trust causes insecurity in relationships. If you're overly protective of her, she'll assume you don't trust her enough to make the right decisions. Unless she wants to date her father, she probably wants to make her own decisions. So let her. You're not going to always be around her, so if you become jealous every single time she's out by herself, you're setting yourself up for a really bad breakup.

Being Too Materialistic

The worst insecurity in relationships is too materialistic. If you're so worried about what you wear or own to impress her, then there's a problem. Not only do you lack confidence in your relationship, but much likely depend on your income to keep your relationship. This isn't good because your income is crucial to your survival. Relationships come and go. Can you afford to do the same with your income? Didn't think so. Buying a nice watch or nice clothes is not a bad thing. However, don't depend on these items to impress her. Instead, impress her with your knowledge as long as it's not money-related.

Being in a relationship seems nerve-wracking at first, but it always is fun if you are confident in yourself. There are many obstacles to overcome, yet couples still enjoy being together with all these challenges. Overcoming insecurity in relationships is never easy but remember there are two of you, so if you are indeed insecure, solving the issue as a team shouldn't be hard.

Blaming

Let's start by recognizing how unpleasant accepting blame or accountability may be. It's tough for most of us to experience the humiliation, sadness, and helplessness that comes with doing anything that makes another person's life difficult or hurts them. It's worse if the other person is someone we care about! This is a pain that we would like to be free of.

So, for us, what psychological purpose does blaming others serve? We don't have to feel the discomfort of those terrible feelings as much when we transfer responsibility away from ourselves. It feels much more empowering right now to get furious at someone else by finding fault with them, whether the problem is real or not. That's what I mean when I say a balm: blaming someone else gives us a momentary reprieve from feelings of inadequacy and self-judgment that we don't want to feel.

Consider what it's like to be the one who is held responsible. Consider the last time you were held responsible for something, whether rightfully or incorrectly. The emotions are the same ones we discussed at the start: embarrassment, helplessness, grief, and hurt. Blaming someone else is an attempt to shift the burden of our painful emotions onto someone else.

However, if we're working together and I shift the blame from myself to you, we're no better off as a group. We're in worse shape for a variety of reasons. Regardless of the effort to throw it off, I'm probably still in pain, and imposing it on you has added to our mutual sorrow. In a partnership, it is uncommon for one person to assume sole responsibility.

Blaming our partner might set off a chain reaction of hurt because anger is typically the easiest element of hurt to feel and express. Both sides attempt to shift responsibility to the other in this (really vicious) loop, but the consequence is a vicious loop of agony. What I mean by a bomb is the shifting of responsibility as well as the circle of agony. It's disruptive; no one wins, and everyone suffers as a result. It's one of the most typical factors we observe blowing up marriages as couples' therapists. If the balm helps at all, it's just for a short time and ultimately makes things worse, making it a pseudo-balm.

Furthermore, blaming yourself harshly isn't particularly useful. At the very least, the toxin isn't being disseminated visibly. However, if you mope, sulk, act the martyr, or publicly criticize yourself, you are still poisoning your surroundings, which will almost certainly affect your relationship.

Balanced compassion and understanding are the finest antidotes. Compassion for yourself to alleviate those guilty, powerless feelings, as well as compassion for any qualities of your relationship that you find challenging. Compassion entails accepting suffering, admitting that we're all flawed and make mistakes, and going toward (rather than away from or against) the suffering in a gentle, loving manner.

Contrary to popular thought, self-compassion allows us to accept more responsibility and perform better than a severe self-punitive approach. The key to curing shame is taking responsibility and being candid about our imperfections (which we all have). It allows us to stay in or improve our relationships instead of flailing to avoid painful feelings, pushing one another away, and feeling alienated and alone.

Replace the pseudo-balm bomb in your arsenal with compassion – compassion for yourself and compassion for your lover!

Playing The Victim

People use Self-victimization (also known as playing the victim) for various reasons, including trying to control or influence other people's thoughts, feelings, and behaviors, justify their abuse of others, seek attention, and cope with situations. They would not seize the opportunity to avoid being victimized because they want to play the victim character and look to others and themselves as victims. The following are the primary characteristics of persons who choose to portray the victim role:

• They are prone to verbally or physically manipulating or abusing people, blaming the other person (i.e., the true victim) for initiating the abuse.

• They manipulate or control the sympathy of others to acquire compassion or support.

• They develop friendships or intimate ties with persons who mistreat, insult, or disrespect them to persuade themselves and the rest of the world of their awful situation.

• They avoid taking responsibility for their lives, blaming others for their abuse or unlucky circumstances instead.

• They spend a lot of time contemplating and talking about other people's greed.

While in the company of the victim personality, keep a lookout for the following:

• Their crippling reliance on friends or coworkers for support and sympathy can be taxing, and you never know if your compassionate replies and efforts are appreciated.

• They can make you feel enraged and aggressive, especially if you discover you were tricked into apologizing to them when it should have gone to the true victim of their abuse.

• They instinctively pull out people's compassionate, loving, and protective instincts, only to manipulate or exploit them.

• They'll occasionally go to lengths to gain attention, such as emptying a spouse's bank account, feeling neglected, and then blaming other people for doing so.

There aren't many advantages to the victim personality, but there are two ways you can gain from it:

• They can make us feel significant and worthwhile. They will always require your assistance with something since they believe they are incapable of taking care of their requirements.

• They want to be trusted; therefore, they'll go out of their way to keep their commitments or finish any chores you assign.

Do you Play the Victim?

You're playing the victim if you frequently:

• Justify your hostility toward others by feeling they are deserving of it.

• Refuse to accept blame for your happiness or sorrow — the world is a nasty place, and no one can be trusted completely.

• Put yourself in situations where others mistreat you to justify your victim status.

• Harass, complain, harass, and beg them to comply with your demands.

• Use the words "You're the only one who can help me" frequently.

• You may go to extremes to exact retribution for perceived or actual mistreatment, such as trashing your property and falsely accusing someone else.

• Instigating hostile conduct in others while downplaying or disregarding your part.

• Be concerned about the prospect of having a beneficial impact on your own life without the help of others.

What Should I Do If I Come Across a Victim?

It will feel good at first to be a part of their happiness and joy, but after a while, you will begin to avoid their childish dependence. They will feel violated if you cut links with them, and the cycle will continue. Remember that self-victimizers have always played a role that has benefited them. A victim can be assisted to change by empathically and regularly challenging them and accentuating those non-victim elements that you enjoy. Asking a question that helps victims reassess their circumstances, such as "you say he became hostile," is an example of empathically challenging a victim. "What happened right before he went berserk?" Statements such as "I admire it when you display this optimistic attitude" exemplify praising the individual's non-victim attributes. It is appropriate for you."

Being Jealous

Are you prone to jealous outbursts when it comes to your boyfriend or husband? Do you want to discover what makes you envious of other people? How do you get rid of your enmity? What steps should you take to stop being envious?

It can be difficult to keep a partner or husband pleased if you are a jealous person. Jealousy tends to make other people unhappy, so you'll need to figure out how to manage this aspect of your personality. Continue reading to learn how to avoid being envious.

Understand why you are Jealous

The key to stop being jealous is to realize why you are jealous in the first place. Most people are not trying to make you jealous, but this trait comes from feeling insecure about your relationship and yourself. When you feel jealousy coming on, it will be important to slow down and understand what has triggered this feeling. As you work on what causes the jealousy, you will probably find yourself changing into a better form of yourself.

Self Esteem

Having high self-esteem is essential to control your jealousy. When you feel good about yourself, it is harder to find a reason to be jealous. Make a list of the things you enjoy about yourself and what makes you happy. Refer to this list every day or when you feel jealous about something. If insecure thoughts creep back in, do what you can to push them out of your mind. Over time you will see your confidence in yourself building, and you will have fewer jealous moments.

Stop Comparing

One of the easiest ways to stop being jealous is to stop comparing yourself to everyone else. You might be compelled to compare yourself to your boyfriend's previous girlfriends to determine who is prettier or funniest. For example, you never need to stop this cycle. No one can be compared like that, and you need to realize that your boyfriend is now with you and loves you for being you.

Put Yourself in the Shoes of Others

While you are comparing yourself to others, you might want to slip into their shoes. Chances are, their life is not nearly as perfect as you believe it to be. Everyone has issues, and some are better at hiding them than others. However, once you step into their shoes, you might find that there is nothing there to be jealous of at all. So, rather than being jealous of others, be grateful for what you have and your lover.

Jealousy Doesn't Help Anything.

Another way to stop being jealous is to realize that this trait doesn't help anything. On the contrary, it usually makes things worse as you will change the way you are around your boyfriend. Jealousy is not pretty on anyone, and eventually, you may find yourself ruining a really good thing. Try to be and act positive and push any negative thoughts from your head. While you can do this, it may take time, and eventually, you will stop being jealous.

Among the seven deadly sins, jealousy is one of the most terrible vices. Jealousy pervades every person's life at some point. And those who have been captured by jealousy will suffer as a result. Jealousy inevitably destroys someone's life prospects, no matter how bright they are. To pass through life in a healthy, sane state, one must understand the rules of "how do you stop being jealous?" Jealousy may be harmful to both jealous individuals and those who are victims of someone else's jealousy; thus, it is critical that you understand, at least in part, how to stop being jealous.

Jealousy can infiltrate your life in a variety of ways, and no amount of self-control will be able to stop it. So, in those cases, the correct and only thing to do is learn how to quit being jealous. While there is an unimaginable number of reasons why you may feel jealous, and they may be incredibly powerful, you must nevertheless attempt to uncover every possible avenue to help you cease to be jealous. For example, how do you resist getting envious when your sister receives a larger Christmas present than you? How do you stop being envious when your friend gets a far higher grade than you, even though you studied? Or, how do you stop being envious when the person you were in love with expresses his respect for another girl? How do you avoid getting envious when you see someone wearing a stunning pearl necklace that your parents did not purchase for you? How can you stop being envious when you can no longer fit into your high school trousers but your friend can? How do you avoid being envious when someone else at work receives praise for something you assisted him or her with? When someone more successful than you is continuously rising the ladder of achievement, why would you be jealous?

Being jealous is truly an integral part of any person's life; however, getting consumed by jealousy is perhaps one of the worst things that you can do. It will not only botch up your tasks but also make your life difficult. Jealousy has never got anyone anything except trouble. Jealousy makes any person bitter to his or her very core of being and ruins his or her relationships with other people. It is thus very important to know that it is a part of life, but how do you stop being jealous is what you should also know.

Fearing Rejection

In love, life and business, we fear many things—loss, Success, Failure, Pain, etc. So, you can see the limitations people have. But not many people know why we fear them. Social Dynamics has uncovered a lot of the reasons why.

In terms of love and relationships, we only have two definite purposes. Survive and Replicate/Replication, and each sex has a resistance. The male has a first-minute resistance because his brain is hardwired to the way we lived 30,000 years ago. We are hardwired that way because 30,000 years ago, we lived in a tribal society of about 100 people. Now let's make this a little easier; you live in this tribe called Quest. Your tribe is of about 50 people, 25 male, 25 female. Now take away the males except you. Then systematically remove the females who are too old, too young, married, pregnant, kids, etc. You are then left with about three women whom you can mate with.

So, what's first-minute resistance. This only occurs in the male - you, as the male, would feel like going up to these women or one of them to try and court them into being your partner. Now you feel this resistance, often known as Approach Anxiety, because your mind has "Survival" set in there and if you were to approach one of these women. Their brother/father/your competitor or other male see you will try to fight you and die. So, your survival instinct says, "Run." But say you overcome that first barrier but run into the second barrier, displaying low value. Women are attracted to a higher value, meaning if a male comes preselected, it shows he is the leader of men, confident, and a fun, friendly personality. These are a few things that a woman looks for. So, if a male displays a lower value of himself, then the woman may not mate with him and leave. So, this further increases his fear because the women who are single and at the age to mate with him would tell each other, and you, the male, will possibly lose any chance of replication.

Now with women, they look for Survival, so the male can assure that they want them. They have a last-minute resistance; the reason for this is because they want a man that will be there for them. If the male they have chosen to mate with seems to portray, "I'm here only to mate with you." For women, the way mating works is they will be pregnant, which is their hardwired mind's reaction. Today we have contraception and so on, but the brain is still hardwired to that old way, so that's why last-minute resistance takes place.

So the reason we fear rejection here, for men, we can't replicate and possibly believe we never will, which is stupid because the population of the earth is at a huge mass. For females, it's fear of the male impregnating them and leaving them; that is the fear that is explained in social dynamics.

In business, it's similar; we think if a prospect rejects our opportunity there rejecting us. We feel that is because of the same reason, except we feel we will have someone kill us if we approach someone with a business idea. This is all because our mind wants to survive. Now you can replicate here as well but not like physically; you replicate your business and success.

To conclude, we fear rejection because of our survival instincts. They guide us, but we can't be complete if we don't take action and speak to people. This serves us if used properly, but we end up feeling down and reject because it's not usually used correctly.

Always Having The Last Word

I often say that I like being correct. And I'm not afraid to argue my points when I know I'm correct. But now and then, I decide that it's time to drop an argument or topic because neither side is willing to move, and the last thing I want to do if it's not a business matter is to thrash a dead horse. So, in those situations, I've got to learn to let someone else have the final say and go on.

I have to admit that type of thing took a little while to learn how to do outside of business. If it's a fact-based discussion, I'll usually find my way into proving my point, and lucky for me, I'm correct more often than not. I rarely take a strongly positive position if I'm not completely sure or reasonably sure of something.

When it gets into talking about opinions, though, I've learned that everyone has their idea of what's "right," and because we all come from different backgrounds and see things from a different point of view, unless it's something that will impact me greatly (such as discussions of race and inferiority/superiority) I've learned that it's not worth the consternation in trying to get someone to see things my way.

In job scenarios, on the other hand, I may go the additional mile here and there to make my point. That's because I'm frequently in a situation where if I'm wrong, it might negatively influence business, and who would ever believe me again? As a consultant, you will occasionally be accurate twice or incorrect twice. If you argue a point, give up, and are later proven correct, you still bear responsibility for not persuading the person you were correct in the first place. On the other hand, if you express your view and then demonstrate that it is true, you may or may not receive credit, but you will not be condemned for being accurate.

Even as a manager, there are moments when you have to allow someone to have the last say. Of course, not when it comes to procedures, especially if you know you're accurate, but when it comes to actions and the like. Sometimes, you could be required to tell someone that they are doing something incorrectly, and they may not appreciate it. You will not benefit from a yelling match with anyone, especially someone who reports to you. Instead, you conduct your business as it should be conducted, let the individual vent and maybe be shown as foolish and unfit of the position, and make no contribution. If you get agitated and try to go toe-to-toe with someone else, you could easily say the wrong thing; it's always easier to maintain the moral high ground when you can.

Is it always simple? No, it isn't. However, it is occasionally the best course of action, especially if you have other things to do.

HOW TO OVERCOME RELATIONSHIP INSECURITY

When two people become a couple, there is always a chance that one of them will be more reactive to the behavior of the other, especially if he lacks the needed self-esteem. Let's pretend an insecure person is a man for the sake of this post. However, if you are a woman, you can still learn and implement this because many of the principles discussed here apply to both sexes.

In a relationship, it is usually acceptable for the woman to show her insecure side (seriously, what woman hasn't done that?), but the same can't be said about the man.

Male insecurities in relationships are considered extremely unattractive and oftentimes the main reason why women leave men. Sure, women love it when a guy shows his vulnerable side (from time to time), but being insecure isn't a good long-term strategy and not a turn-on for her.

Relationship insecurities are frequently the result of deep-seated personal concerns. It's not like men become insecure as soon as they enter a relationship. Men who are insecure in all of their relationships are insecure as a whole. They usually hope that the female will fix them in the way that "she inspires me to be a better person!" but this rarely happens.

To overcome your insecurities, you have to improve your overall situation. The first step is to learn why you turn into this insecure mess when you start dating a beautiful girl. Is it because you always doubt yourself? Or because you can't imagine what she is doing with you in the first place? Or is it because you constantly think that she might cheat on you?

So, let's dig a little bit deeper and find out how to overcome insecurity in relationships.

This should come as no surprise that an insecure man's main issue is his negative attitude. His faulty mentality is what causes him to lack the necessary self-esteem. It's his faulty attitude that causes him to open out to the lady about his insecurities. But, in the long run, it's his faulty thinking that puts the partnership in jeopardy.

The problem is that a man with this perspective is exceedingly needy and desperate for a woman's devotion. He can't face the notion of her being taken away from him. It's as if losing her is the same as losing his identity. His lover is the only person who can help him with his deep-seated issues. As a result, he gets reliant on her and feels unfinished without her.

This is also when his anxieties generally start to show, and the girl realizes that the charming, great guy she fell for couldn't even retain his sanity - how can he assist her when she needs it? As you could expect, an attitude like this will drive her further away from him.

So, what's the answer? How do you deal with insecurity? Simple! You must alter your viewpoint!

You must understand that a woman desires a man who does not require her (I did not mean "desires"). With this approach, he shows that his happiness is not dependent on women and that he has other things that make him feel better. Therefore, a man who does not require the company of ladies to be happy is appealing.

For an insecure man, this is by far the most important piece of relationship advice. He can probably fix most of his insecurity issues by focusing on other things that make him happy rather than putting his girlfriend on a pedestal.

You'll have to establish your source of happiness rather than depend on your partner to do it for you if you're serious about overcoming relationship instability. This also implies that you must eliminate bad actions that are detrimental to the relationship. Don't waste your time attempting to gain her approval! Stop being so possessive and selfish! Stop monopolizing her time and attention!

Never put your trust in your girlfriend to make you a better person; she can't. You are the only one who can truly make a difference. She can only properly point you, and you must allow her to do so.

I wish I could tell you that conquering your anxieties is a simple process that you can learn quickly and easily, but that is not the case. Instead, it is a process that requires you to change your mindset about many things, and therefore it takes time.

I've seen people with a lot of ambition, excellent potential, and wealth who fail to realize their dreams because of their anxieties. Even if the scenario and circumstances are ideal, if you do not feel safe inside yourself and are constantly unsure of yourself, you may not recognize that you are the roadblock to your ambitions; you prevent yourself from becoming successful in life. Only you, however, can conquer your insecurities.

Some signals reveal your insecure self, and being aware of them can help you spot them in yourself and others.

• Overtly apologetic: An insecure individual lacks a healthy self-concept and constantly doubts himself or herself. Everything spoken or done is tinged with self-doubt and hence becomes apologetic very quickly.

• Having trouble accepting compliments: Compliments are difficult for insecure people to accept. As a result, they tend to dismiss compliments since they believe they are genuine and do not know how to receive them gracefully.

• Defensive behavior: An insecure person becomes extremely defensive at the first suggestion of criticism or punishment. As a result, insecure individuals have a difficult time overcoming criticism.

• Misunderstood sense of humor: Insecure people tend to make fun of themselves in all of their uneasiness, frequently to the point where it is obvious to others that they have low self-esteem.

• Avoiding making decisions: An insecure person avoids making decisions because they are afraid of being held responsible if something goes wrong.

• Not asking for help: Insecure People have a hard time asking for aid. They avoid requesting help when they need it because they are afraid of being rejected.

To overcome insecurity,

• Take a chance: Have faith in yourself and your ability. Even before you begin a project, a relationship, or a task, believe that you will do well, speak well, and achieve your goals. Faith gives you the power you need without you having to do anything.

• Develop healthy behaviors: Examine your habits and determine which ones are caused by insecurity. Change your habits and build positive ones that will help you achieve your objectives and ambitions. With practice, you'll notice that your new healthy behaviors benefit you and eventually become a way of life.

• Adopt a positive mindset: Think positively, force yourself to see the bright side of every situation, and challenge your beliefs and attitudes. Even if you feel insecure for a small moment, you will notice that good thoughts will quickly follow and begin to encompass you.

• Take care of yourself: groom yourself, look in the mirror, and talk to yourself. Looking nice indeed contributes to feeling well. Take care of yourself since a healthy body and mind are both necessary.

• List everything you want to do: Make a list of your issues, worries, and insecurities. Break down the actions or things you need to perform to overcome your anxieties into manageable goals. Tick items off as you finish them; this will boost your self-esteem. As a reward, do something you enjoy to encourage yourself to keep on with your dream fulfillment.

Maybe it's you, or maybe it's your partner. In any case, your relationship is filled with uneasiness and may be on the verge of breaking up. So how do you re-establish trust and a firm foundation so that your relationship can thrive and grow?

First, recognize that feeling uneasy or not quite ready to trust in a relationship after being harmed in the past is entirely natural. But this does not necessarily mean your relationship will be insecure.

Everything boils down to one thing: trust. Insecurity is a result of a lack of trust, which might be real or imagined. Therefore, rebuilding trust is the best method to overcome insecurity in a relationship.

As you've probably heard from various sources, trust takes time to develop. However, you may not be aware that the key to establishing trust in a relationship is transparency.

What is transparency, and how can it be used to reduce relationship insecurity?

Transparency, when broken down, means being entirely open and honest with your partner about what you're doing and what they may expect from you. If a lack of trust is the result of hidden motives and deeds, then transparency results from bringing everything into the open.

Transparency entails informing your spouse ahead of time that you will be working late. Transparency entails informing your partner when you're going out to dinner with pals to catch up. Finally, transparency expresses your views and puts an end to all the half-truths and missionary lies that straddle the slippery line between honesty and lying.

Because this is a two-way street, both you and your partner must be transparent. If only one partner is expected to act transparently, it becomes a form of punishment or shame rather than a means of bringing the two of you closer together.

And you'll have to wait a while to see the outcomes you want. There will be no overnight miracle. Trust takes time to develop, and both you and your partner will need to be committed to sticking it out through the early phases while you wait for the findings.

To get started, it's a good idea to sit down with your partner and honestly address your relationship's emotions of uneasiness. Then, discuss how you both want to change things and work together to create a realistic code of transparency that you can agree to follow.

It may not be simple to re-establish trust in your relationship, but with persistent effort and dedication on both sides, you and your partner can put an end to feelings of uneasiness. Practice being more open and honest about what you're doing and feeling in your daily lives, and be prepared to put up the work to keep it up and build your relationship.

STEPS TO OVERCOMING SELF DOUBT

Self-doubt is a powerful emotion. It has the potential to change the way you think about a range of things, including your relationship. When we are filled with uncertainty and insecurity, we are quick to judge ourselves harshly, subject ourselves to unattainable standards, and wonder why we are deserving of love. Self-doubt, if left unchecked, may be hazardous, if not disastrous, to a relationship's health.

So, what are your options for breaking free from your shackles? How can you overcome the (mostly internal) obstacles that prevent you from being happy? The first step is to recognize the emotion. The following are the next twelve:

1. Quit claiming to be insecure.

This is a crucial step: if you're currently focusing on better yourself, especially your sense of security, you're essentially rewriting your story. This is impossible if you continue to define yourself as "an insecure person" or if you ponder about your various confidence issues regularly. After you've eliminated the negative thoughts, you can begin to alter your behavior.

2. Put your doubts to the test.

The second phase entails putting some distance between yourself and these negative emotions. They may appear to come from within you, but they are essentially an external presence that you may investigate, scrutinize, and eventually erase. Begin to recognize that your doubts are your greatest anxieties surfacing and disguising themselves as actual opinions. They aren't. They are untrue. Unless you give them power, they have none.

3. Give your critic a name.

Not with a name like "Dave" or "Josephine" (though you certainly can), but with a name that helps you recognize those thoughts when they start to seep into your self-awareness. If you're gazing at a photo of you and your significant other and thinking to yourself, "They're so much more attractive than me, I'm sure people notice and wonder why we're together..." Then instantly pause and realize that THAT is your critic's voice, not your own, your partner's, or anybody else's.

4. Don't overthink things.

Overthinking is a no-win situation. If you dwell on a bad thought, it will appear more serious and pervasive than it is. Overthinking will find you a negative or insecure notion if you don't already have one. It's not a good habit in general because it causes worry, anxiety, and tension within oneself, but it spells doom in the context of your relationship.

5. Get to the bottom of the problem.

Understanding that you have insecurities is merely the first step; the hard work begins after that. What important is that you figure out why. Think about how long you've been dealing with these difficulties. Is it feasible to trace it back to when you were a kid? Friends? Exes? Asking tough questions of yourself and taking an inventory to understand where these feelings come from will offer you a lot of information and a clearer path to safety.

6. If you require assistance, don't be afraid to ask for it.

Assume you discovered that your apprehension stems from something deeper, such as past trauma or buried experiences from the preceding phase. In such scenario, you owe it to yourself to process those feelings properly. For assistance, see a therapist or psychiatrist, or join a support group. If you discover that your insecurities are more serious than you believed, this is a crucial step to take.

Take the first step in receiving the help you need. Download Relish to get limitless 1-on-1 relationship coaching from a qualified relationship coach.

7. Don't make any more comparisons.

When we compare ourselves or our relationships to others, we are setting ourselves up for disappointment. Because it's in our nature, it's impossible to kick this habit of cold turkey merely. But we have control over how much of it we are exposed to! Simply reducing your time spent on social media can help you achieve this aim.

8. Develop self-assurance.

Self-confidence is the best antidote to self-doubt. How do you make more of it a reality? Keep a nightly journal in which you write down one thing you did that day that you are proud of, then read the last few entries the next morning. What could be a more motivating way to start the day?

9. Allow yourself to be open.

No couple on Earth can read each other's minds, no matter how in sync you are with your mate. Rather than crossing your fingers in the hopes of telepathy, try opening up the avenues of communication. Being vulnerable not only strengthens your bond with your partner but also allows them to acquire insight and understanding into your path. It's a win-win situation.

Allow one of our relationship coaches to create a free, personalized lesson plan to improve your communication skills. Now is the time to install.

10. Improve self-talk.

Realizing that you have control over your self-talk is one of the most effective methods to counteract negativity. And some of the best advice on the matter is quite straightforward: As though you were conversing with a close friend, speak to yourself. You wouldn't say anything like, "You're correct, I don't think you're worthy of love," would you? "How dare you think that?" you'd say. You're incredible! You're great. There is no one like you on the planet."

11. Surround yourself with positive people.

You should have a little more free time now that you've cut back on your social media usage, right? Use it to surround oneself with positive things and people. You're said to be the product of the five people with whom you spend the most time, so take a quick mental inventory of the people with whom you choose to spend your time. Address negativity if you notice it.

12. Accept insecurity as a normal aspect of life.

This is an extremely significant topic, even though it may seem counterintuitive. Excessive self-doubt is harmful to your confidence and your relationship. But, on the other hand, a little insecurity is only one of the costs of being human. The ups and downs can make you believe you're the only one who feels that way, but the truth is that we've all been there. And we'll all be back there.

Even though self-doubt can feel like being swept into a maelstrom of uncertainty and gloom, climbing out is surprisingly simple. The consequences are obvious if you truly practice each of these stages with intention, going through them chronologically as many times as necessary. You'll feel more at ease. You'll have fewer doubts about yourself. You'll still feel those feelings now and then (you're only human, after all), but they won't influence your decision-making or your sense of self. You'll be able to see what your lover sees in yourself.

CHAPTER 7: THE ATTACHMENTS STYLE: WHY IT IS DANGEROUS, WHERE IT COMES FROM AND HOW TO OVERCOME IT

Why do babies cry when removed from their mothers? We're wired for attachment. Based on our mother's actions and later experiences and other conditions, we develop a style of attachment that shapes our behavior in close relationships.

Most people, fortunately, have a secure attachment since it helps them survive. It ensures that we are safe and capable of assisting one another in a dangerous situation. The fear we experience when we don't know where our child or a missing loved one is during a crisis, as depicted in the film "The Impossible," is not codependent. It's perfectly natural. Like a baby worried about its mother, frantic calls and searches are labeled "protest behavior."

Attachment Styles

We seek or avoid intimacy in a range of ways, but whether we're dating or married for a long time, one of the following three patterns is most common:

50 percent of the population is safe.

Twenty percent of the population is anxious.

25% of the population is avoidant.

Secure-Anxious or Anxious-Avoidant combinations account for 3-5 percent of the population.

Secure attachment. Warmth and love flow effortlessly, and you may be intimate without having to worry about the relationship or little misunderstandings. You accept your partner's flaws and treat him or her with respect and love. You are direct and able to openly and assertively discuss your wins and losses, wants, and sentiments without playing games or manipulating others. You're also aware of your partner's requirements and make an effort to accommodate them. You don't take things personally and don't react to criticism since you have high self-esteem. As a result, you don't become defensive in confrontations. Rather, you de-escalate the situation by fixing problems, forgiving, and apologizing.

Anxious Attachment is a term used to describe a feeling of attachment: You desire intimacy and are capable of it. You give up your demands to please and accommodate your partner to preserve a positive bond. However, if your requirements are not addressed, you will be unhappy. You're preoccupied with your connection and acutely aware of your partner, fearful that he or she wants less intimacy. You have a proclivity for taking things personally and imagining bad scenarios. This may be explained by brain abnormalities discovered in those who have anxious attachments.

To seek attention and comfort from your partner, you can play games or manipulate them by withdrawing, acting out emotionally, not returning calls, inciting jealousy, or threatening to leave. You can be envious of his or her focus on others and phone or text frequently, even if you've been requested not to.

Attachment avoidance. Your independence and self-sufficiency are more essential to you than connection if you shun contact. You can appreciate intimacy up to a point. You act self-sufficient in relationships and aren't comfortable revealing your sentiments. (For example, in a study of couples saying their goodbyes in an airport, avoiders showed less touch, fear, and sadness than others.) You keep your independence and put off committing. Once you've committed, you create mental distance by focusing on your partner's minor shortcomings, reminiscing about your single days, or fantasizing about another idealized relationship.

As someone with high attachment anxiety, you are hypervigilant for any signs that your partner is trying to control or limit your autonomy and freedom. Flirting, making unilateral decisions, neglecting your partner, or rejecting his or her feelings and needs are all examples of distancing behaviors. Your partner may say that you don't seem to need him or her or that you're not open enough because you hold secrets or don't express your emotions. In truth, he or she looks to need you regularly, but this makes you feel powerful and self-sufficient in comparison. You are unconcerned about the end of a relationship. When the relationship is in jeopardy, though, you convince yourself that you don't have attachment needs and hide your sorrow. The problems aren't that the needs don't exist; they're that they're suppressed. Alternatively, you may get apprehensive since the prospect of intimacy no longer poses a threat.

Relationships

Even persons who are self-sufficient when single are frequently astonished to find themselves dependant once romantically coupled. This is because intimate interactions unconsciously activate your attachment type, as well as your earlier experiences of trust or fear. It's very normal to grow overly reliant on your mate. You feel safe when your needs are addressed.

Your partner's style can be determined by their actions and their response to a direct request for deeper intimacy. Does he or she strive to fulfill your expectations, or does he or she become defensive and uneasy, or does he or she give in once and then withdraw? Someone secure will not play games, will communicate well, and will be able to compromise. Someone with an anxious attachment type might welcome more closeness, but they still need assurance and worry about the relationship.

In relationships, anxious and avoidant attachment styles resemble codependency. They describe the emotions and behaviors of pursuers and distancers, which I've already discussed. Each is unaware of their wants, which are communicated by the other. This is one of the reasons behind their attraction to each other. Those who pursue anxiously are frequently uninterested in those who pursue securely. They are most likely to attract someone apprehensive. Although it is painful and makes people more anxious, the tension of an insecure attachment is energizing and familiar. It validates their feelings of desertion in relationships, as well as their ideas about not being enough, lovable, or safely loved. Distancers require someone to pursue them to meet their emotional needs, which they mostly ignore and are not supplied by another avoider. Pursuers and distancers, unlike those who are permanently committed, are not adept at resolving conflicts. They often get defensive, attacking or withdrawing, exacerbating the confrontation.

Pursuers and distancers alike become sad and empty without the chase, conflict, or compulsive behavior resulting from their unpleasant early ties.

Changing Styles

Although most people's attachment styles do not change, you can adjust yours to be more or less secure based on your experiences and conscious effort. Seek treatment and interactions with individuals capable of a secure attachment to transform your style into one that is more secure. A secure attachment type makes you feel more secure, while an anxious attachment type makes you feel less. This will assist you in being more secure. Healing from codependency and changing your attachment style go hand in hand. The following are involved in both:

• Heal your shame and boost your confidence. You will be able to avoid taking things personally as a result of this.

• Develop assertiveness.

• Learn to recognize, honor, and communicate your emotional demands assertively.

• Take a chance on being genuine and direct. Play no games or try to sway your partner's feelings.

• To become less faultfinding, practice accepting yourself and others - a difficult task for codependents and distancers.

• Learn to resolve disagreement and compromise from a "we" perspective rather than reacting.

Pursuers must take more responsibility for themselves, while distancers must take more responsibility for their relationships. Instead of a codependent relationship or alone with a false sense of self-sufficiency, the result is a more stable interdependent partnership.

Because persons who have a solid attachment are more likely to be in a relationship, there are more avoiders among singles. They aren't looking for an ideal, unlike avoiders; thus, they don't stay lonely for long when a relationship fails. This makes it more likely that anxiously attached daters will date avoiders, reinforcing their negative outlook on relationship outcomes. Furthermore, nervous people bond fast and don't take the time to consider whether their partner is capable of or willing to fulfill their needs. They tend to focus on the qualities they have in common with each new, idealized spouse and ignore possible issues. They repress their wants to make the relationship work, giving the wrong signals to their spouse in the long run. Attaching to an avoider becomes more likely as a result of all of this behavior. Pursuers mistake their need and concern for love when their partner withdraws, rather than seeing that the problem is their spouse's unavailability, not themselves, or anything they did or could do in the future to change that. Instead of embracing the facts and cutting their losses, they persevere and try harder.

People worry that being dependent on someone would make them more dependent, especially after exiting an uncomfortable codependent relationship. When there isn't a stable attachment in a codependent relationship, this may be true. Healthy dependency, on the other hand, permits you to be more interdependent in a stable connection. You have a safe and secure home base from which to travel across the globe. This is also what allows toddlers the confidence to individuate, express their actual selves, and gain independence.

Similarly, patients in treatment often fear becoming too reliant on their therapist and quit as soon as they start to feel better. This is when their dependency issues surface and need to be addressed - the same worries prohibit people from having solid attachments in relationships and drive them to seek out someone who avoids them. On the other hand, good therapy provides a safe bond that allows people to grow and become more autonomous, rather than less. Here's the paradox: when we rely on someone else, we can be more self-sufficient if the relationship is solid. Another reason it's difficult to change on your own or in an uneasy relationship without outside help because it's difficult to change without it.

The origin of the concept of attachment

In the initial years of our lives, our idea of ourselves evolves from the symbiotic unification of the mother and baby. With time, we realize that we are different from our parents. First, we realize that we have a detached physicality, and finally, we construct an identity originally formed on the responses given by our parents.

As we grow older, we achieve developmental assignments and gain individuality, but we also realize that we can never again unite with another physical body like our mothers. We may affiliate with other people and search for imminence, but it will always be from the point of beneficial distance.

No one can straightforwardly understand another person's reality. If we want another person to know us, we should be in touch with him. This can be both hard and irritating as we want our partners to understand the way we want to be understood and corroborate our thoughts and ideas by agreeing with us.

But everyone has their thoughts and understanding of life, which makes them live in their world different from ours. An obvious understanding and acceptance of this difference is the real beginning attachment with the other person.

The method of wanting to be acquainted with the other person initiates the understanding of attachment. Irritation and disputes are part of this method, and those people who understand this thing are more apt to work on this method.

It is highly important that if we want to attach ourselves with another person, then we should first attach ourselves to our "self" because to accept another person's difference, we should first come to terms with our difference, or else we will search for combination, and not attachment.

To receive higher levels of attachment, we should build up an independent value of ourselves, meaning that we should be aware of our value even if another person is not telling us. This is care for ourselves.

If we are too reliant on what others will say about us, we will never be happy unless another person comes and says something nice about us. True attachment is not the shared respect of society; it is one soul getting to know another. Attachment is the conclusion of two different souls trying to understand, accept, and accept.

The Science of LoveHow did Harlow go about creating his love science? He took newborn monkeys from their mothers a few hours after birth, then arranged for them to be "raised" by two types of surrogate monkey mother robots, both of which could dispense milk. One mother was constructed entirely of bare wire mesh. Another was a wire mother covered in lovely terry cloth. Harlow's first finding was that monkeys with a choice of moms spent considerably more time clinging to the terry cloth surrogates, even while their actual feeding was provided by bottles mounted on the bare wire moms. This demonstrated that newborn love was more than a mere response to physiological requirements being met. Hunger and thirst were not the primary motivators for attachment. It was impossible to limit it to nursing.

Then Harlow tweaked his experiment and discovered something else. When he divided the monkeys into two groups and gave them no choice between the two sorts of moms, they all drank the same amount of milk and grew at the same rate. The parallels, however, ended there. Monkeys who had soft, tactile contact with their terry cloth mothers acted very differently from monkeys with cold, harsh wire mothers. Harlow theorized that members of the first group benefited from a psychological resource inaccessible to members of the second group: emotional attachment. Cuddling kept newborns' growth on track by offering reassurance and security.

What did Harlow see that convinced him that emotional attachment made a significant impact on development? When monkeys raised by terry cloth surrogates were startled by unexpected, loud things like teddy bears playing drums, they made physical contact with their moms, rubbed against them, and eventually calmed down. Harlow theorized that they used their mothers as a "psychological base of operations," allowing them to stay playful and curious after the initial shock had passed. When monkeys raised by wire mesh surrogates were afraid, they did not flee to their moms. Instead, they hurled themselves on the ground, gripped each other, rocked back and forth, and screamed in terror. According to Harlow, these actions were strikingly similar to the actions of autistic and impoverished youngsters commonly seen in institutions, as well as the disordered behavior of adults confined to mental hospitals. The incredible power of attachment and loss over mental health and illness has never been more forcefully demonstrated.

Despite the fact that Harry did not coin any concepts, he made a significant contribution to the Attachment Theorem.

The attachment system is a connection theory.

What if you're in a relationship with someone who was emotionally uninterested in you? What if you were dealing with someone who was emotionally draining?

After one or two relationships with someone who possesses either style, people give up on finding "the one." Self-doubt sets in, and you start to believe that "there is something wrong with me."

To comprehend this phenomenon, you must first comprehend attachment theory, which is one of the most well-researched ideas in relational psychology. Our early relationships with a major caregiver, most typically a parent, shape our expectations for how love should be.

How well these caregivers were present and responsive to our bodily and emotional needs shaped our perceptions of ourselves and others. Our romantic partners in adult relationships stimulate our attachment system.

The alarm for the attachment

What causes us to be triggered? Consider your primary caregiver's availability.

• Were they unreliable, inattentive, or always there for you?

• When you had an issue, who did you turn to?

• Was someone there that you could rely on?

You can start identifying your attachment type by studying the four adult attachment types and how they often affect couples' relationships.

According to attachment theory, if a caregiver was attentive and available to you as a child, making you feel safe and secure, you have a secure attachment type. To have a good relationship, it is necessary to develop a stable attachment. Your partner in a safe relationship is always there for you and has your back. If you have an insecure personality (or choose someone who has an insecure personality), you will be triggered all the time and never feel safe or comfortable in your relationship.

You develop an uneasy attachment pattern if your caregiver is unresponsive. There are three basic manifestations of an insecure attachment style.

Anxious Attachment develops when a caregiver's responsiveness and availability are uneven, leaving the youngster unsure of what to expect. This person can be clinging as to an adult and has a hard time trusting their relationship.

When a caregiver is inattentive, avoidant attachment develops. These children prefer to play alone and believe that no one is there to fill their demands. They usually describe themselves as self-sufficient as adults.

Disorganized Attachment: This type of attachment develops due to abuse, trauma, or disorder in the household. A youngster develops a fear of the caregiver and lacks a true "safe base."

All of these personality types impact how you act in romantic relationships and how you find a love partner.

So, can one modify their attachment style to a more secure way of relating to this?

Changing the way you attach

Yes, but it will take a lot of effort. Therapy can be extremely beneficial in many cases. It's critical to be conscious of your attachment style and the partners you choose. A good therapist will help you gain the awareness needed to determine whether you're reacting to old hurts.

In maturity, we tend to repeat problematic interpersonal behaviors from our childhood. The familiarity, as much as many loathe it, is reassuring. You could even confuse the familiarity of your early life experience with the sense of romantic chemistry.

Choose a partner with a stable attachment style and work on growing yourself in that relationship to challenge your anxieties. By confronting your worries about love, you can develop new attachment styles that will help you maintain a meaningful, loving relationship.

A child's initial bond is formed before he or she reaches the age of seven months. Although some infants are incapable of bonding, almost all infants will attach to someone. Attachment is typically limited to one or two major people, generally parents. These attachments typically endure a lifetime, and future attachments are compared to early attachments throughout a person's life. Although the mother plays the major attachment function, the father also has a significant part to perform. Although it is uncommon for the roles to be reversed, fathers give an additional stimulation and object attachment source for their children.

A dyadic interaction is assumed in attachment theory. The relationship's two parts are complementary to one another. The caregiver is as attached to the child as the child is to his or her parents. Most of the time, the two collaborate to keep the vicinity and understand what is safe. The child will follow the parent if the parent moves away, and the parent will follow the infant if the infant moves out of reach. The existence of both members is required for the attachment to existing. It's just as vital to be absent as it is to be there. Separation anxiety, detachment, and a sense of loss can occur when the caregiver is not there. The cornerstone of attachment is separation trauma and the experience of loss of the most significant person in the infant's life. The infant's reaction to the loss confirms or refutes his or her preconceived notions, and it may cause him or her to change their mind about the caregiver.

The attachment relationship varies from one family to the next and from one parent-child dyad to the next. There are three main types of attachment for infants, each of which makes the bonding experience more or less pleasurable. Type B infants use their primary caregiver, usually their mother, as a safe base from which to explore their environment. The securely linked infant walks away from the mother freely yet takes frequent looks in her direction to analyze her whereabouts. The baby is unaffected by others picking him up or putting him down, and he goes away to play. As a result, the infant rapidly recognizes where the primary caregiver is with them. The infant is fussy at first when the mother leaves them but soon calms down since they know the mother will return. Depending on the child's age and stage of development, separation can encompass both physical separation and emotional rejection or separation—one area of attachment theory research in attachment styles.

Anxiety-avoidant (Type A) and anxious-resistant/ambivalent attachment styles are two types of insecure attachment patterns (Type C). Type A babies show their uneasiness by avoiding the mother's sight, failing to seek proximity, and avoiding her gaze. They are less distressed when the caregiver leaves them than other types, and they do not want to re-contact when the caregiver returns. Anxious-resistant babies show their insecurity by opposing their mothers while clinging to them. They are demanding and difficult to calm down. They scream uncontrollably when left with a stranger. They may be angry with their mother for her absence and cling to her when she returns. When Type A babies perceive a lack of compassion from their caregivers, they learn to suppress their emotions. Type C babies cannot comprehend the sporadic nature of caregiver interactions with them and become hypervigilant, constantly looking for loss and abandonment. An instance of physical separation or emotional rejection is supposed to stir the infant's rage and hatred, leading to furious thoughts and acts. Dread and anxiety of being further rejected and losing the attachment figure grow due to this fear antagonism.

As part of social interaction, the child's attachment is influenced by the caregiver's manner. Infants who are securely bonded to their moms are more likely to have mothers who are affectionate, caring, and responsive to their needs. Type A mothers are insensitive to their babies' signals, rarely make close physical contact, and have frustrated and hostile reactions toward their children. In their interactions, Type C mothers are hesitant and hesitant. They aren't as affectionate as Type A mothers, but they aren't as rejecting. There's some indication that caregivers picked up their parenting style from their parents. One interesting discovery is that mothers of secure-attached children are more likely to have been secure-attached as infants.

The link between a child and the main caregiver is the most crucial event in developing a child's personality. It's where the youngster gets his or her sense of safety, self-esteem, and self-control. However, the consequence of a first relationship is significantly more than just emotional. It has an impact on how effectively a youngster recalls, learns, and interacts with others. A child's brain is wired in a specific pattern by a secure bond (or its lack thereof).

How can one feature of early childhood have such sway over a person's life? And how do child psychologists come to their conclusions regarding attachment? Both questions are answered in this section.

Although John Bowlby (1907-1990) conducted his naturalistic observations of youngsters more than half a century ago, subsequent research has further strengthened psychologists' loyalty to his viewpoint. Bowlby was a British physician and psychotherapist who agreed with Freud's core concept that a person's early childhood experiences are crucial in forming personality. Bowlby examined the individual interactions that lead to a secure or insecure early attachment between a mother and her child to Freudianism in great depth. And he used etiology to make evolution the organizing principle for explaining how these interactions arise from both mother and child's survival instincts.

It's all in the way they smile.

How could anyone be able to resist such a face? Most adults find a baby's smile and kewpie pie cheeks charming. Bowlby explained how this visual attractiveness works as a wonderful adaptation (similar to infant cubs, kittens, or birds), almost ensuring that a newborn will receive vital care, comfort, and nourishment. Meanwhile, a mother's instincts to care for and protect her child are usually enough to motivate her to participate in this mutually beneficial connection.

Babies have a huge repertory of very effective signals to ensure they receive what they need to survive and develop, which Bowlby dubbed the "human attachment system." They cry and fuss when they aren't smiling, or they coo and clutch at their mother's face, hair, and breasts when she isn't smiling. They also follow her about the home like a duckling does when following its mother through tall grass.

Babies are friendly by the age of 3 months, but they usually save their biggest smiles for the significant caregiver in their lives; adults who mirror these smiles right back. By calling these behaviors adaptive, Bowlby made the point that they are inborn. The baby's purpose, he said, is to stay physically close to the most important source of his independent survival.

Bowlby noted that newly hatched geese and ducklings develop a preference for the first moving object they see, a process called "imprinting." Similar to these birds, human newborns prefer moving objects and often recognize their mothers within days of birth. However, full bonding on the part of a human baby takes much longer than other animal species, at least six months longer than a duckling. Fortunately, human parents usually pick up any slack in the bonding process. After only a few minutes with a newborn, mothers and fathers typically say they're goners, already "in love." It sounds pretty adaptive, doesn't it?

Attachment and Locomotion

A baby's attachment to a key adult, generally her mother, should be solidified by the sixth or seventh month. Bowlby discovered that this timing correlates with the commencement of a baby's crawling in another nod to ethology. This suggested that autonomous locomotion was linked to the conclusion of the baby's bonding process, which began at birth. Of course, a newborn takes much longer to crawl out of his crib than a chick does to leave the nest. Before chicks and toddlers venture too far from "home base," instinct ensures that they know its whereabouts. Safety and exploration are the two competing goals in a baby's earliest years. A child who stays safe survives; a child who explores develops the intelligence and skills needed to grow successfully.

These two needs often oppose each other. This is why Bowlby and his successors believe that a child develops an internal "thermostat" to monitor his level of safety in the environment. When he gets too far from home base, an internal alarm bell sounds.

It's a common scenario: a child wanders away from his mother (either crawling or "toddling") until an inclination compels him to turn around and see if she's still there. He may continue if she is still where he left her. Alternatively, he may return to check-in before continuing his exploration. By internalizing what Bowlby called "functioning models" of their carers, the attachment bonding process allows toddlers to control their wants to explore or cling to that specific adult. In the preceding case, one such working model is "It's all right. If I crawl any further, Mom will be there." "I can't go too far because she might leave me [el] it's too scary," for example—babies from one of two models as a result of their mothers' actions over time.

The Rhesus Monkey Experiments

Striking images of some very unhappy, even self-destructive monkeys convinced many doubters about the importance of early animal and human mother-child bonding in the 1950s. These photos came from Harry Harlow's (1905-1981) famous series of Rhesus monkey experiments. Harlow separated a group of infant monkeys from their mothers and raised them with two types of substitute mother figures. One was made of bare wire; the other had a soft cloth cover over a wire form. Harlow's research questions were:

1) Would infant monkeys form attachments to the inanimate mother substitutes?

2) Would they receive any observable emotional comfort from either kind of substitute mother?

The infant monkeys form an attachment, but only with the cloth-covered wire mother surrogates, not the uncovered wire forms. Interestingly, both types of surrogates provided food by way of a bottle attached to the wire. This told researchers that the bonding they observed between the infant monkeys and the cloth-covered surrogates was not solely based on nourishment. Something else was behind the bonding.

The baby monkeys in Harlow's experiments habitually clung to the cloth-covered wire "mothers" in a manner strikingly similar to how they would hold on to a real monkey mother. The experiment provided a convincing demonstration that the critical ingredient in attachment formation is not food but "contact comfort." Because they were gentler to touch, these softer surrogates were the next best thing to a mother monkey.

Harlow's results altered the psychoanalytic view of how the mother-child bond is formed, making skin-to-skin physical contact as important as the oral gratification received by newborn babies while being nursed or bottle-fed by their mothers. Harlow's study also went against the position of the behavioral theorists who emphasized food itself as the primary reinforcer of a baby's behavior.

Harlow's rhesus monkey experiments strongly inferred that serious negative consequences occur when a human baby is deprived of a strong bond with a mother figure in the first year of life. Bowlby then confirmed this hypothesis with his observations of children in post-World War II orphanages.

Other insights gleaned from these experiments concerned the long-term negative impact on the monkeys' emotional and physical health due to this deprivation. To compensate for a missing mother, these monkeys would suck obsessively on their bodies. They remained huddled in corners, rocking themselves, with distant looks in their eyes. Later, when placed with other monkeys, they became hostile, aggressive, and rarely mated.

Later experiments with other monkeys helped clarify the importance of timing for human mother-baby attachment patterns. Monkeys who spent at least three months with their mothers before being separated showed less severe behavioral abnormalities than those separated from birth. Monkeys separated from their mothers at the age of 6 months showed no long-term negative behaviors. Researchers concluded a sensitive or critical period for bonding between monkey mothers and infants, which lasts for six months. In humans, this critical period is believed to last three years, with any deprivation suffered in the first year of life considered the most harmful.

Making a Secure Attachment

Even with mother and child instincts and parental awe to move things along, attachment is not an instantaneous process that begins and ends in the delivery room. It's more like a dance that begins before birth and continues throughout a baby's first year. Although a baby's primary attachment object is normally the mother, the chances are just as good that whoever gives regular and caring care of a baby - whether a father, grandfather or adoptive parent - might build the same secure bond with that baby. Factors that increase a secure attachment include:

1) A single primary, regular caregiver for the baby's first six months, rather than a series of irregular caregivers.

2) Synchronized routines for eating, sleeping, and stimulation with that caregiver, especially during a baby's first few months.

3) Consistent smiling, touching, and affection by the primary caregiver.

4) Acting consistently in response to the baby's distress with comfort, warmth, and competency.

A caregiver's sensitivity to a baby's distress is important, but too much of a good thing is counterproductive. Research shows that when super-attentive mothers responded instantly to their baby's every gurgle, cry, and hiccup, their children became less securely attached. The lesson: children react poorly to smothering. It hampers their independence and inhibits the process of learning to self-soothe.

The Chemistry of Attachment

Another perspective on attachment is revealed by the biochemistry behind parent-baby bonding drives and behaviors. Using brain scans and tests of hormone levels and heart rates, researchers can now see the biochemical results when a secure attachment is made and when it fails to take place.

A Mother's Chemistry

A woman's hormones prepare her for giving birth and then ready to feed and nurture a newborn baby. When she is pregnant, her brain circuits are rewired, and her senses focus on caring for a newborn. As a result of her evolutionary instincts that manifest in this intense chemical preparation for childbirth, she will focus nearly all of her attention and energy on this tiny person until its survival is assured.

For humans and throughout the animal kingdom, the hormone oxytocin is fundamental to the first mother-child bonding after a baby is born. Many animal research help elucidate the role of this hormone in human relationships. Female rats and sheep (ewes) given oxytocin injections will even take care of young rats and young lambs they've never seen before.

A mother's uterine contractions trigger the brain to release a flood of oxytocin and the neurotransmitter dopamine in human labor and childbirth. The pain-suppressing effects of these hormones are essential after a woman has experienced anywhere from 6 to 36 hours of labor. When the baby is born, they create a residue of euphoria as chemical flooding peaks in the first minutes following birth[md], often coinciding with the first time the newborn is put to his mother's breast for suckling.

It is well known that a mother who has decided to have her baby adopted should not touch the infant because the act of touching and smelling the baby causes her to release oxytocin. This causes many mothers to reconsider their decision to make an adoption plan.

During the last month of pregnancy, a mother-to-be starts producing the hormone that prepares her for nurturing and lactation: prolactin. This hormone causes milk to be secreted from her breast. Oxytocin assists by enabling the milk let-down response in a woman's breasts and sensitizing the new mother to her infant's touch. The baby's touching of his mother's breast with his hand or lips causes oxytocin to be released. During nursing, oxytocin surges, bringing pleasure and relaxation to the mother and deepening the mother/baby bond.

A Father's Chemistry

The latest studies have shown that when a man becomes a father, his brain goes through changes, too. Soon after hearing the news that he's about to be a father, a man starts to produce cortisol, a stress hormone. Cortisol levels spike around four to six weeks after a man hears the big news, and then they decrease as the pregnancy progresses. Then, about three weeks before the baby arrives, his testosterone levels fall by about 30 percent, making him more cooperative, less competitive, and more likely to show his softer side.

For men, the hormone vasopressin plays a key role in preparing for a baby's birth, helping them make the emotional connections required by new fatherhood. Also, during the last few weeks of his mate's pregnancy, a man's prolactin level rises by 20 percent. It's not clear what effect prolactin has in a man, but it is thought to impact his falling testosterone levels indirectly. After his child's birth, his estrogen level, a nurturing influence that is normally very low in a man, increases. The point of these changes appears to be to make fathers more maternal in their behaviors, at least more than their normally high levels of testosterone will allow. A man's hormone levels begin to return to normal about six weeks following birth. A man's oxytocin production is triggered by higher estrogen levels and frequent skin contact with his infant—all of this chemistry aids in reinforcing a father's newly snuggling and cooing habits.

At the same time, fathers and mothers interact with infants and toddlers in different ways. A father is more likely to bounce or rock kids in a joyful, rhythmic manner, whereas women soothe and contain them with hard or mild caressing. As children get older, a father's attitude to their physical care becomes more rough-and-tumble, and he becomes more difficult and less compassionate than a mother. Both approaches are beneficial and required for developing youngsters, according to research. When a mother and her infant create their primary connection during their infant's first six months, research has shown that they both begin to build far closer relationships with their dad and siblings soon after.

Chemistry of Insecure Attachment

Like her mother, when a baby receives affection and loving attention, she enjoys the calming effects of oxytocin. A lack of nurturing touch early in her life can create a negative neurochemical pattern in her brain based on those early disappointments. With negative expectations brought to future attachments, this child may react to increased oxytocin caused by physical or emotional intimacy with fear, not with anticipation of pleasure.

Stress hormones are activated instead of the warm and cuddly feelings induced by oxytocin. The chemical cortisol, which keeps us alert and helps us deal with stress, appears to be the main culprit at work here. Cortisol is sometimes required, such as in the morning when its concentration is highest, to help us wake up. When you want to be calm and open to human connection, cortisol's dampening effect on oxytocin is less favorable. In a baby's first year, one of these lifetime good or negative metabolic patterns emerges.

Attachment Styles

In the 1970s, psychologist Mary Ainsworth built on Bowlby's attachment theory by creating a now-famous series of controlled laboratory experiments with mothers and babies, called the "strange situation" experiment. The goal of these experiments was to figure out the detailed patterns and styles of behavior that cause either a secure or insecure parent-child bond.

Two concepts are central to these experiments:

1) Stranger anxiety - Wariness or fear of unfamiliar adults, shown by most infants between the ages of 6 and 24 months

2) Separation anxiety - Distress that infants between 6 and 24 months experience when separated from their primary caregivers

Normally anxiety is not viewed as a positive experience. But in the case of children younger than three, fears toward strangers and separation from a mother are healthy and appropriate responses. They provide evidence of a child's positive, secure relationship with a mother or other primary caregiver.

Ainsworth scripted eight episodes to test mothers' and babies' responses to certain stresses to closely observe attachment behaviors between mothers and babies in a more controlled setting. The dual focus throughout is on the baby's response to the mother's absence and the presence of a stranger and the mother's responses to her baby. Ainsworth's now-famous and commonly used "strange situation experiment" involves 1-year-old babies and mothers from various backgrounds and ages.

The Strange Situation Experiment

There were eight stages in Mary Ainsworth's strange situation procedure. After each stage listed next, the behavior of a securely attached baby is noted. Stages two through eight last about three minutes each:

1) Introduction - An assistant introduces the mother and baby to the room while the mother holds her baby. 30 seconds.

A mother holds a calm baby.

2) Unfamiliar room - Baby is on the floor with toys available to play with, and mother sits nearby.

Baby may be wary of the new room but uses mother as a base of security, maintaining eye contact with her while playing with toys.

3) Stranger enters - An unfamiliar female knocks, enters the room, speaks with mother, and then goes to play with the baby.

Baby may show "stranger anxiety" and prefers mother to play with a stranger. While the mother is present, the baby may allow a stranger to approach and play nearby.

4) Mother leaves - quietly, leaving the baby with a stranger who goes and sits in mother's chair.

The baby shows separation anxiety and renewed stranger anxiety. May accept some comfort from a stranger but wants mother back.

5) Reunion of mother and baby, stranger exits. A mother comforts her baby. And if the baby wants to continue playing with toys, does so.

Baby seeks contact and comfort from mother. The baby clings to the mother. The baby may continue to play after receiving comfort.

6) Mother leaves again, saying "bye-bye" on her way out, leaving the baby alone.

The baby shows renewed separation anxiety and distress.

7) Stranger enters again, joining baby who is still alone, sits in mother's chair, then calls or goes to the baby.

The baby may show more anxiety toward the stranger and prefers that mother returns.

8) Reunion of mother and baby, with mother picking up baby and stranger leaving.

There's a joy for the baby upon reuniting with the mother. Baby wants to hang on to mother.

Observing Attachments

Ainsworth found that secure attachment relationships tend to be associated with mothers who hold their babies frequently and with mothers who hold their children long enough so that they appear satisfied when they're put back down. Securely attached babies are aware of their mother's whereabouts and confident that she will return after leaving the room. If they're distressed, securely attached babies usually obtain quick comfort after being held by their mothers. Other qualities of a secure mother-baby attachment include:

1) Mother is sensitive to calls and signals of distress from baby and responds quickly.

2) Mother goes along with the interactions and games that baby initiates.

3) Mothers adjust the baby's feeding and sleeping schedules according to the baby's rhythms.

4) The relationship is mutual, not dominated by the needs and moods of the mother.

Based on her observations, Ainsworth concluded that "indifferent parenting" led to insecure attachments between mothers and babies. Other researchers have subsequently added data from observational studies to show that obtrusive and over-stimulating parenting styles can also lead to insecurely attached babies.

Mothers of insecurely attached babies were found to be anxious and irritable frequently. The most extreme of these mothers showed little interest in their children, mechanically handling them, and behaving otherwise resentfully toward their babies.

Four Attachment Styles

Ainsworth formalized a system for rating attachments from thousands of controlled observations of mothers and children using four categories.

1) Secure /65 percent - Uses mother as home base; prefers her to a stranger; may show distress at her leaving; seeks physical contact when reunited with mother.

2) Insecure-avoidant / 20 percent - Doesn't prefer mother to a stranger; avoids contact with mother when reunited.

3) Insecure-resistant / 10 percent - Shows ambivalence toward mother; seeks contact, then

resists it; doesn't avoid contact with mother; some show anger; some are passive.

4) Insecure-disorganized / 5 percent - Acts confused or dazed; maybe calm, then angry;

often will remain motionless; shows apprehension; sometimes is resistant or avoidant

Whether avoidant or resistant, insecurely attached babies learn that their caregivers will not respond sensitively to their needs. As a result, they may reject their mother's attempts to comfort them by looking away or showing anger and frustration in times of stress.

Babies who exhibit insecure-disorganized attachments sometimes have parents who are neglectful or abusive. Often, researchers found that these parents had unresolved difficulties with their parents and may have been abused as children. Their pregnancies were often unplanned and unwanted. In less severe cases, disoriented insecure behavior can occur when a mother displays anxiety or sends mixed signals to her baby.

Obstacles to Attachment

The most often-cited obstacles when developing a secure attachment are the quality of the mother's caregiving and the compatibility of the baby's temperament with the mother's temperament.

Maternal Depression

Depressed mothers often miss and ignore a baby's signals of distress. They also have a harder time entering into a synchronous relationship with their child. With a depressed mother, babies first become angry at their mother's lack of attention and responsiveness, perhaps crying harder and for longer periods. But over time, these babies begin to match the mothers' depressive symptoms. As mentioned earlier, by the age of 6 months, babies internalize a specific working model of their mothers as either responsive or nonresponsive, and their brains rewire to reflect this experience.

According to statistics, 13 percent of pregnant women and new mothers experience situational depression due to becoming a mother. The hormonal shifts can aggravate any existing low-level depression or susceptibility to it, added stress, and sleeplessness that accompany having a baby. Post-partum depression is an insufficiently recognized factor that can inhibit the development of a secure attachment in a baby's first six months.

In a pioneering study at Columbia University, psychiatric epidemiologist Myrna Weissman showed that when mothers of grade school children were successfully treated for depression, the depressive symptoms in a significant percentage of the children also dramatically improved. The study's key finding is that depressed children's improvement came without direct treatment of the children.

Mismatched Temperaments

It takes two people - an adult and a baby - to form a secure attachment. Stella Chess described three different expressions of temperament: "easy," "slow-to-warm-up," and "difficult." A friendly "easy" baby who is more likely to approach than withdraw from a novelty in her environment has been found to have an easier time becoming "securely attached." A "slow-to-warm-up" baby requires more inducement to draw into a relationship. A "difficult" baby requires more time.

Some recent research has leaned a more integrative approach to the question of which factor is most likely to inhibit attachment: the quality of a mother or other primary figure's caregiving or the baby's possibly difficult temperament. The major finding was that the quality of caregiving a baby receives is most predictive of whether the child forms a secure or avoidant attachment as measured in a strange situation test. However, the baby's temperament appears to determine which type of insecure attachment is formed. Temperamentally fearful children tended to form resistant attachments, where they kept their distance from their mother but protested strongly. More outgoing babies with unresponsive mothers formed avoidant insecure attachments where they protest less but were content to ignore the mother in favor of a stranger.

Babies are just as likely to form secure attachments with fathers as mothers if the father is the primary caregiver. Summing up the data from studying 710 babies in 11 studies, the percentage of secure versus insecure attachments was 65/35 for fathers and 65/35 for mothers. The type of attachment formed also tended to be alike from one parent to the other.

Is Early Attachment Destiny?

The existing research shows that babies who form secure primary attachments to their mothers in the first year turn out better, meaning they display more favorable development outcomes later in childhood. Here's a sampling of that research.

Securely attached children at age 12 to 18 months, when measured at two years of age, were found to:

1) Be better problem solvers.

2) Be more complex and creative in their symbolic play.

3) Display more positive and fewer negative emotions.

4) Be more popular with their playmates.

Each of these findings was made in a controlled setting, comparing 2-year-olds who benefited from secure attachments to those found to be insecurely attached to their primary caregivers.

Longer-term studies paint a similar picture. Children who have been securely linked to their careers at the age of 15 months were re-examined in follow-up studies between 11 to 12 and 15 to 16. Among the findings were the following:

1) Those who had been securely attached as toddlers were described at the older ages as socially more popular, more curious, and self-directed.

2) Those insecurely attached at 15 months were socially and emotionally withdrawn and less interested in learning. They also tended to be unenthused about surmounting challenges.

These studies showed that the type of secure or insecure attachment between parent and child in the first few years tends to be the same in the child's grade school and high school years. Other research has shown that a secure relationship with another person - father, grandparent, adoptive parent, or daycare provider - can somewhat offset the negative consequences of a poor attachment with a mother.

John Bowlby used the term "working models" to describe how young children internalize their earliest relationships to emphasize that a child's working models could change. They could improve (or deteriorate) due to later relationships with teachers, romantic partners, or close friends. But even with these caveats, don't fail to understand the importance of a baby beginning life with a secure bond to a significant adult.

Attachment and Working Mothers

Although many people would like to hear a definitive statement about daycare's positive or negative effect on young children, there are few absolute or simple answers to this question. However, there is evidence for parents to consider when making individual decisions.

From the research:

1) Separations from working mothers and placement in daycare generally do not prevent babies from establishing a secure primary attachment. This is true if the mother and father are sensitive and responsive caregivers when they are home with their child.

2) Babies younger than six months placed in full-time daycare face an elevated risk of forming an insecure attachment, and, in one study, they had lower scores on school readiness at 36 months.

3) One large nationwide study found that time spent in daycare added to the risk of a child's forming insecure attachments only when combined with mothering that was less sensitive and less responsive.

4) High-quality daycare helps buffer young children from the negative effects of being separated from their parents.

5) Even when daycare is less than optimal, a child's outcome depends more on the quality of care received at home.

6) A mother's attitudes toward working outside the home and placing her baby in daycare are extremely important in shaping the attachment she forms with her child. Any sort of resentment negatively affects the mother-child bond.

Suppose there's an ideal scenario to be garnered from the existing data. In that case, it is this: a mother with a positive attitude who spends the first six to seven months as a full-time, stay-at-home mother stands the best chance of forming a secure attachment with her baby.

Of course, public policy and business practices are not as supportive of mothers making this choice in the United States compared to other Western countries. Using the same measurements discussed in this chapter, those societies that provide longer paid maternal and paternal leave and supply subsidized childcare have higher securely attached children. In Great Britain and Sweden, 75 percent and 74 percent of babies were securely attached, compared to 64 percent in the United States. For low-income Americans, the number of securely attached babies is 50 percent.

The Least You Need to Know

1) Attachment between babies and a significant adult is an instinctual process with life-long implications.

2) Within a secure attachment, a baby finds safety and the will to explore her world, developing an internal thermostat to keep both in balance.

3) Babies and mothers in "strange situation" research studies are rated on four different styles of attachment that range from a secure attachment to avoidant, resistant, or disorganized insecure attachments.

4) Babies younger than six months in full-time daycare are at higher risk of developing an insecure attachment than babies with at-home mothers.

How do attachment styles affect our relationship as adults?

Attachment styles or types are defined by the behavior displayed in a relationship, particularly when the relationship is threatened. When faced with relationship troubles, someone with a secure attachment type may be able to discuss their feelings and seek support openly. Insecure attachment styles, but on the other hand, may become needy or clingy in their most intimate relationships, act selfishly or manipulatively when vulnerable, or just avoid connection entirely.

Knowing how your attachment style molds and influences your relationships can help you understand your behavior, how your partner views you, and how you react to intimacy. Identifying these patterns can then assist you in clarifying what you require in a relationship and the best strategy to resolve issues.

While the newborn-primary caregiver connection shapes attachment types significantly, especially during the first year, it is crucial to emphasize that attachment strength is not exclusively determined by the quantity of parental love or the quality of care that newborn receives. On the other hand, attachment is based on the nonverbal emotional communication that develops between caregiver and infant.

An infant expresses its emotions through nonverbal cues such as crying, cooing, and, later, pointing and smiling. The caregiver, in turn, analyzes and interprets these signs, responding to the child's demand for food, comfort, or affection. A secure attachment emerges when this nonverbal communication is successful.

Attachment success is unaffected by socioeconomic criteria such as wealth, education, ethnicity, or culture. Adulthood does not correlate with insecurity when it comes to attachment style. Your personality and your intervening experiences during childhood, adolescence, and adulthood can all influence your attachment type.

Types of attachment

Aside from defining attachment as secure or insecure, there are subcategories of insecure attachment that result in four major attachment styles:

• Stable attachment

• Ambivalent (or anxious-preoccupied) attachment

• Avoidant-dismissive attachment

What is the appearance of a secure attachment style?

People with secure attachment are more empathetic and capable of setting appropriate boundaries, and they feel safer, more stable, and more fulfilled in their relationships. While they are not afraid to be alone, they usually flourish in intimate, meaningful partnerships.

The impact of stable attachment style on adult relationships

Having a stable attachment style does not imply that you are perfect or do not have relationship troubles. However, you are probably secure enough to accept responsibility for your faults and inadequacies, and you are willing to seek help and assistance when necessary.

• You value your self-worth and can be yourself in an intimate relationship. You are at ease expressing your emotions, hopes, and needs.

• You enjoy being with people and openly seeking support and comfort from your partner, but you do not become unduly concerned while the two are apart.

• You're equally content for your partner to rely on you for assistance.

• You can maintain emotional equilibrium and seek healthy ways to manage disagreement in a close relationship.

• You are robust enough to recover from disappointment, disappointments, and tragedy in your relationships and other facets of your life.

Primary caregiver relationship

As someone with a secure attachment style, your primary caregiver was likely to stay involved with you as an infant while efficiently managing their stress and calming and soothing you when you were distressed. They consistently made you feel safe and comfortable, connected with you through emotion, and responded to your shifting needs, allowing your nervous system to become "securely linked."

Of course, no parent or caregiver is flawless, and no one can be entirely present and attentive to a newborn 24 hours a day, seven days a week. In truth, establishing safe attachment in a child is not required. However, if your caregiver missed your nonverbal indications, they probably continued to try to find out what you needed, thereby keeping the safe attachment process on track.

Because of the solid basis of a healthy attachment bond, you were able to be self-confident, trustworthy, hopeful, and comfortable in the face of conflict as a youngster.

Whether you have an ambivalent or anxious-preoccupied attachment style, you may be concerned about being overly attached or your constant craving for love and attention. Alternatively, you may be worn down by dread and concern about whether your lover truly loves you.

• While you seek connection and intimacy with a significant other, you have a tough time trusting or relying on your partner.

• Being in a romantic relationship can take over your life and cause you to become overly focused on the other person.

• You may struggle to set boundaries, interpreting space between you as a danger that might cause panic, anger, or worry that your spouse no longer wants you.

• Because of your fear of loss, you can react violently to any perceived threat to the connection.

• You are uneasy or jealous when you are separated from your partner and may resort to guilt, control. You tendanipulative measures to keep them close.

• You require regular reassurance and lots of attention from your spouse; others may criticize you for being overly needy or clingy, and you may struggle to maintain close relationships.

Relationship between primary caregivers

Your parent or primary caregiver was most likely uneven in their parenting style as a baby, sometimes involved and sensitive to your needs and other times inaccessible or distracted. This inconsistency may have left you uneasy and unsure whether your needs in this "first" relationship would be met and serve as a model for your conduct in subsequent relationships.

The attachment style is avoidant-dismissive.

Adults with such an avoidant-dismissive insecure attachment style contrast sharply with those who are ambivalent or excessively fixated. Instead of desiring intimacy, they are so afraid of the contact that they shun emotional connection with others. They would rather not rely on others or be reliant on others.

The impact of avoidant attachment style on adult relationships

You may find it challenging to accept the emotional connection if you have an avoidant-dismissive attachment style. Because you value your individuality and freedom so much, intimacy and closeness in a romantic relationship may make you feel uneasy, if not strangled.

• You are an independent person who is content to care for yourself and does not believe you require the assistance of others.

• You're uncomfortable with your emotions, and partners frequently accuse you of being aloof and walled off, stiff and intolerant, the more someone tries to be close to you or the needier a partner becomes. In response, you accuse them of being overly dependent.

•

To recover your sense of freedom, you may belittle or dismiss your partner's sentiments, keep secrets from them, indulge in affairs, or even abandon relationships.

You may prefer short-term, casual relationships to long-term intimate ones, or you may seek equally independent partners, keeping their emotional distance.

While you may believe that you do not require close connections or intimacy, the truth is that we all do. Humans are hardwired for connection, and even those with an avoidant-dismissive attachment style desire a close, meaningful relationship if they can overcome their deep-seated anxieties of intimacy.

Relationship between primary caregivers

An avoidant-dismissive attachment style is frequently the result of a parent who was inaccessible or rejecting during your childhood. Because your caregiver's needs were never satisfied on a consistent or predictable basis, you were forced to detach yourself and try to self-soothe emotionally. This laid the groundwork for later in life avoiding closeness and desiring independence—even when that independence and lack of closeness creates its misery.

In primary relationship, people communicate using one of four Attachment Styles: Each of these styles has unique qualities and vulnerabilities. Secure, Anxious, Avoidant, and Fearful-Avoidant are the four personality types. The following three styles are all versions of insecure styles, but they express that uneasiness differently. This part provides a brief overview of what to know about the characteristics of the Anxious person and what to do if your Anxious attachment style is impeding your dating or relationship success.

Keep two things in mind while you read: First, no one is completely one style or the other. Most of us are a combination of one or more styles. Thankfully, this is the case. That provides us some leeway in figuring things out! The other style can develop in response to the style of the person you've met. In other words, if the person they meet is more anxious than they are, an anxious person may recede and appear more avoidant. Both kinds are insecure and react to the discomfort they both experience with intimacy and connection.

FAILURES OF AN ANXIOUS STYLE

Except in the scenarios described below, people with an Anxious personality tend to discover someone they like and are eager to get into a relationship. When they are with their lover, their anxiety lessens; when they are separated, their anxiety increases. Even unintentional "misses," such as calling later than promised or, worse, not calling until the next day, increase worry. They are frequently giving with their time and energy and accommodating to their partner's demands. It is critical to have arrangements for the next get-together, and they will be apprehensive if their spouse has not presented anything. They may make certain that something is booked, or they may be reluctant to propose the next date for fear of placing too much strain on the relationship and waiting anxiously for the other person to call them. Preoccupation with what I call "relationship evaluation" is one of the most upsetting aspects of the anxious person's experience. When the anxiety kicks in, they start meditating on prior talks, assessing how the last date(s) went, and worrying that the speed at which they think things will progress may drive their partner away.

Furthermore, they may foresee disastrous outcomes in the connection. This can be excruciatingly painful for the anxious person. Do you recall the part in "Flashdance" where the dancers were working out at the gym, and one of them was stressing over whether or not the man she met would call? That's what we're referring to.

The dating pool is disproportionately weighted with nervous and avoidant persons because the comfortable people are more likely to wade out together. As a result, a nervous person is more likely to encounter someone with an avoidant personality. It's critical to remember that these Attachment Styles are how our "Attachment System" operates. In a nutshell, the "Attachment System" is regarded as a component of our genetic inheritance, a part of us that is critical to our species' existence. The mother and infant must form an attachment to look after the child, and the youngster feels afraid of being too far away from the mother. Because human newborns and children cannot fend for themselves, such a link boosts the child's chances of reaching adulthood. We create a style that sticks with us as the "way of the world" due to several variables from our early attachment experiences. When two adults meet for a romantic relationship, their attachment types interact, and their "Attachment System" becomes active. This is where the anxious individual may encounter difficulties.

THE ANXIOUS AND AVOIDANT MEET

When an Anxious person encounters an Avoidant person, the Avoidant person's tendency to maintain a distance can develop a gap that the Anxious person feels forced to close. The switch is flicked in the Attachment System, and people go into overdrive, sometimes mistaking their fixation with narrowing this gap for true love. Indeed, some of the same neurotransmitters are involved in "love." However, this is one of the most difficult things for anxious people to deal with. They believe that because they would not expend so much psychological energy on someone who isn't "the one," it must be love. In actuality, it's occasionally an overactive Attachment System kicking into high gear due to the Avoidant's distance.

This characteristic of worried attention might be exacerbated or alleviated depending on the partner's actions. Secure people can handle an anxious individual's anxiety so that the anxious individual feels more at ease and trusting of the connection. However, an avoidant partner's desire for "space," conflicting messages, and denial of the anxious person's legitimate relationship demands can sustain or intensify the anxious person's concern. Not to mention that the nervous person's pursuit can lead to greater distancing, resulting in the well-known "pursuer-distancer" dance. At this point, the Avoidant is likely to argue that the Anxious person is overly clingy.

SUGGESTIONS FOR THE ANXIOUS INDIVIDUAL

If you have an Anxious personality and interfere with your relationships, here are some key tips. First, recognize and accept your genuine relationship requirements. Ignoring your needs and focusing too much on your partner's expectations does not result in your needs being met, and you cannot be happy in a relationship if your needs are not addressed. For example, if you need to interact with your spouse at least once a day, let them know. It can be frightening to declare your needs, yet the response you receive is critical information. Don't believe the lies that you're too reliant or dependent on. People you date should be judged on their compatibility with your relationship needs, not your capacity to change yourself to satisfy and accommodate them. If you believe you are excessively needy, meaning you are overly reliant on another person to live your life, this is an important issue to address in your therapy. That is not the same as being informed by an avoidant individual that natural cravings for connection are "too needy."

Second, identify and eliminate Avoidant persons early on. People who avoid having any or all of the following characteristics:

1. They communicate conflicting messages. For example, they may express strong interest in you but are just casually seeing someone else, or they may express strong interest in you but are only casually seeing someone else. Take precautions. It's time to move on if you're getting too many contradictory messages.

2. They are looking for the ideal mate. "Imaginary Lover," by the Atlanta Rhythm Section, is a classic. Looking for the perfect person somewhere out there is a great way to miss out on the excellent person right in front of you. Not to mention the fact that there is no such thing as an "ideal" person. We're all flawed individuals with flawed partners. Avoid imagining how you might transform into that ideal person for them, especially if they provide hints that it won't be you. This is an example of adapting to their wants rather than understanding your partnership's demands. The individual who discovers the "ideal match" is likely to be a secure person who overlooks the flaws in another secure person.

3. They desire to meet "The 1," but they always find some flaw in another person or in the circumstances that prevent them from committing. An Avoidant individual would remark something like, "They're perfect but 'geographically unattractive.'" "I enjoy everything about them, except they like opera, and I despise opera!" could be another example. Perfection does not exist. We're all just .79, .82, or .89. Love occurs when the number is rounded up to a "1."

4. They disrespect your emotional well-being and, when challenged with it, continue to do so. If you expose your relationship demands and your partner's answer is to reiterate why they cannot meet your requirements (rather than contemplating how they may), there is a clear problem.

5. They imply that you are overly needy, sensitive, or hypersensitive (thus invalidating your feelings and making you second guess yourself). Don't let this go on for too long.

6. They disregard things you say that bother them. For example, if you say, "It would mean a lot to me if you wouldn't answer your phone throughout dinner," and they continue to answer or text, your needs are less significant than what they are saying. This is also how they deal with their concern about the connection with you. This is one way they may put it up so that you are only "so close."

7. If your messages aren't being received despite your best attempts, take a step back and examine whether enough of your requirements are being satisfied for you to continue working. Remember, no one is flawless, and we all want a second chance to make things right. However, if the list of avoidant actions is too long, it may be best to inform the person and move on.

Third, try dating differently. Be true to yourself and employ good communication. Don't make the mistake of believing you're too needy and compensating for your partner's need for space. Also, don't dodge important dialogues out of fear of alienating them. First, you'll be happier being yourself, and second, you'll know sooner (rather than later) whether this individual is someone with whom you can have a relationship. Probably the most "point-at-able" example is a lady with a limited window of opportunity for childbearing. It would be critical for him/her to interview potential partners early on to determine whether they, too, desired children. It's best to keep looking if he says he doesn't or isn't sure. If having children is essential to you, don't waste your time trying to persuade them to change their minds on such a crucial topic. You don't have to be harsh or critical; express how vital it is to date someone who is similarly eager to establish a family.

Similarly, I recall speaking with a woman who told her date that pets were quite important to her. It was fine if he didn't like dogs; nothing would happen. That's exactly how she felt. That's admirable of her to say that. And congratulations to him! He, too, was a dog lover. They dated, married, and now they constantly rescue and foster dogs.

Fourth, recognize that there is a lot of fish in the waters. Give multiple people a chance before settling on one. Remember that anxious people believe their chances are limited; therefore, they should seize the next opportunity. The dating pool is weighted toward Anxious and Avoidants, but there are also Secure people out there. Continue looking until you locate one.

Fifth, give confident people a chance. Do you recall what we talked about before about the Attachment System? You may feel bored at first since an Avoidant's distance hasn't activated your Attachment System. As a result, the typical exhilaration and tension that puts you at risk of mistaking obsession for love aren't present. That can be strangely boring. Keep in mind that the Anxious person is prone to misinterpreting tranquility in a relationship as a lack of desire. Despite the ending of the Sex and the City films, Mr. Big's avoidance was a constant source of dread for Carrie. In the TV show, how many times did they break up? It's one thing to go for Mr. Big in a comedy; it's quite another to go after Mr. or Ms. Avoidant in real life. Remember that you may meet a very nice person and not immediately detect "chemistry."

If you have an anxious attachment style, these are some helpful hints. Also, keep in mind that humans do not exist in binary all/anything states. Someone may be a little anxious or a little avoidant. Things may work out if you are both old enough to know themselves well and observe and care about your style's impact on the other person. The idea is for both persons to move toward a more secure connection type. And, by the way, fashions change throughout time as a result of relationships. A tumultuous, traumatic relationship will cause a person to become more insecure about their appearance (either more Anxious or more Avoidant). Learning to communicate with each other securely will result in increased security in your relationship, and each of you will develop a more Secure Attachment Style over time. People that are securely attached have three main characteristics: they are available, attentive, and responsive. Security develops as a result of practicing these qualities and witnessing them in your partner.

CHAPTER 8: BUILDING A HEALTHY RELATIONSHIP

Every relationship has its ups and downs, and they all involve effort, dedication, and the ability to adapt and evolve with your partner. There are steps you can take to create a healthier relationship, whether you're just starting or have been together for years. Even if you've had a lot of broken relationships in the past or struggled to rekindle the romance in your current relationship, there are ways to remain connected, find satisfaction, and experience long-term happiness.

What makes a healthy relationship?

Every relationship is different, and people meet for a variety of reasons. Having a shared vision about what you want your relationship to be and where you want it to go is part of determining a successful relationship. And you'll only know that if you have a long and frank conversation with your partner.

There are, however, certain traits that most stable partnerships share. Whatever goals you're working toward or obstacles you're facing together, knowing these fundamental concepts will help keep your partnership meaningful, satisfying, and exciting.

You maintain a meaningful emotional connection with each other. You make each other feel cherished and satisfied emotionally. Being loved and feeling loved are different things. When you're loved, you feel welcomed and respected by your partner, as if they understand you. Some relationships get trapped in a state of peaceful coexistence without the partners emotionally relating to each other. If the relationship may appear to be healthy on the surface, a lack of ongoing commitment and emotional interaction helps widen the gap between two people.

You're not afraid of (respectful) disagreement. Some couples communicate in hushed tones, while others can raise their voices and argue vehemently. However, to have a good relationship, you must not be afraid of confrontation. You must be able to communicate your concerns without fear of retribution, and you must be able to settle disputes without degradation, embarrassment, or insistence on being right.

You keep outside relationships and interests alive. Despite what romantic fiction or movies can say, no single person can satisfy all of your needs. Expecting too much from your partner, in reality, can put undue strain on a relationship. Maintaining your own identity outside of the relationship, maintaining ties with family and friends, and maintaining your hobbies and interests are all valuable ways to stimulate and enrich your romantic relationship.

You communicate openly and honestly. A core component of any partnership is successful communication. When both parties know what they want from the relationship and feel comfortable sharing their concerns, desires, and needs, it will reinforce the bond and increase trust between you.

Staying in love vs. Falling in love

For the most part, falling in love seems to be a natural process. It takes dedication and hard work to remain in love or keep the "falling in love" feeling alive. It is, however, well worth the effort gave the benefits. A strong, stable romantic relationship can be a constant source of comfort and satisfaction in your life, bolstering all facets of your well-being in good times and bad. You can create a lasting relationship that lasts—even for a lifetime—by taking steps now to maintain or rekindle your falling-in-love experience.

Many couples only pay attention to their relationship when they have real, inevitable problems to solve. They often return their attention to their jobs, children, or other interests once the issues have been resolved. Romantic partnerships, on the other hand, necessitate constant attention and dedication to thrive. It will take your commitment and effort as long as a romantic relationship's well-being is important to you. And acknowledging and addressing a minor issue in your relationship now will also help avoid it from being a much bigger issue later on.

The following suggestions will assist you in preserving your first love experience and maintaining a healthy romantic relationship.

Tip One: Spend quality time face to face

You fall in love with each other by looking at each other and listening to each other. You will maintain the falling-in-love feeling over time if you continue to look and listen with the same attentiveness. You probably have fond memories of your first dates with your significant other. All seemed fresh and exciting, and you undoubtedly spent hours simply talking or brainstorming new and exciting ideas to try. However, as time passes, the pressures of work, family, other commitments, and the desire we all have for alone time will make finding time together more difficult.

Many couples note that their early dating days of face-to-face communication are increasingly being replaced by hurried texts, emails, and instant messages. Although digital communication is useful for certain things, it does not positively affect your brain and nervous system as face-to-face communication. It's awesome to give your partner a text or a voice message saying "I love you," but if you don't look at them or have time to sit down with them, they'll always think you don't understand or acknowledge them. As a couple, you'll become more distant or separated. The emotional signals you both need to feel loved can only be shared in person, so create time for each other no matter how hectic life gets.

Commit to spending some quality time together regularly. Take a few minutes per day, no matter how busy you are, to put down your mobile devices, stop worrying about other things, and concentrate on and communicate with your partner.

Find something that you both enjoy doing together; Whether it's a joint hobby, dance class, regular stroll, or morning coffee, there's something for everyone. Try something new together. Trying new things as a family can be a fun way to bond and keep things fresh. It might be as easy as trying out a new restaurant or taking a day trip to a new place.

Focus more on having fun together. Couples are often more playful and friendly in the early stages of a relationship. However, when life's problems get in the way or old resentments start to build up, this playful mindset may be overlooked. Maintaining a sense of humor will potentially assist you in getting through difficult times, reducing tension, and resolving problems more quickly. Consider innovative ways to surprise your partner, such as taking roses home or booking a table at their favorite restaurant on the spur of the moment. Playing with small children or pets will also help you rediscover your fun side.

Tip 2: Stay connected through communication

A good partnership relies on effective communication. You feel secure and comfortable when you have a good emotional bond with your partner. People stop relating when they stop interacting well, and periods of change or stress may exacerbate the disconnect. It can sound simplistic, but as long as you communicate, you should solve any problems you have.

Do not leave it up to your partner to find out what you require.

It's not always straightforward to express your needs. For one thing, many of us don't devote enough time to considering what matters most to us in a relationship. Even if you are aware of what you require, discussing it can make you feel exposed, humiliated, or even ashamed. But see it from your partner's viewpoint. It's a privilege, not a burden, to provide warmth and understanding to those you care for.

If you have been dating for a while, you might presume that your partner knows exactly what you're thinking and what you need. Your mate, on the other hand, is not a mind reader. Although your partner will be aware of your needs, it is much better to share them explicitly to prevent any misunderstanding.

While your partner can sense something, it may not be what you need. Furthermore, people evolve, and what you required and desired five years ago could be very different now. Instead of allowing frustration, confusion, or rage to grow due to your partner's inconsistency, develop the habit of telling them what you need.

Take note of your partner's nonverbal cues

What we don't say transmits a great deal of our correspondence. Eye contact, tone of voice, stance, and movements like leaning forward, crossing your arms, or touching someone's hand convey much more than words.

You'll be able to say how your partner really feels and react appropriately if you can pick up on their nonverbal signals or "body language." To have a good relationship, each person must be aware of their own and their partner's nonverbal cues. Your partner's reactions can vary from your own. For instance, one person may find a hug after a stressful day to be a loving communication mode, while another may prefer to go for a walk or sit and talk.

It's also important to make sure that the vocabulary and body language are in harmony. If you say "I'm fine," but clench your teeth and turn away, your body is indicating that you are not "fine."

You feel cherished and content when your partner sends positive emotional cues, and your partner feels the same when you send positive emotional cues. When you stop caring about your own or your partner's feelings, your relationship suffers, and your ability to interact suffers, especially during stressful times.

Be a good listener

Although our culture places a lot of focus on talking, learning to listen in a way that makes another person feel heard and understood will help you develop a deeper, stronger bond.

There's a huge difference between this kind of listening and just hearing. You'll hear subtle intonations in your partner's speech that tell you how they're feeling and the feelings they're trying to convey if you listen—when you're engaged with what's being said. Being a good listener does not imply that you would consent or change your mind with your partner. However, it will help you recognize common points of view that will aid in resolving conflict.

Tip 3: Keep physical intimacy alive

Touch is an important aspect of human life. The value of frequent, affectionate touch for brain growth has been demonstrated in studies on infants. And the advantages don't stop when you're a boy. Affectionate touch raises oxytocin levels in the body, a hormone that affects attachment and bonding.

Although sex is often a pillar of committed relationships, it should not be the only source of physical intimacy. Contact that is regular and affectionate—holding hands, embracing, kissing—is also necessary.

Of course, it's important to be aware of your partner's preferences. Unwanted contact or awkward overtures will make the other person tense up and withdraw, which is the opposite of what you want. This, like so many other facets of a successful relationship, will come down to how well you and your partner express your desires and intentions.

Even if you have a busy schedule or small children, you can help to keep physical intimacy alive by scheduling daily couple time, whether it's a date night or just an hour at the end of the day where you can sit and chat or hold hands.

Tip Four: Learn to give and take in your relationship

If you plan to get what you want 100 percent of the time in a relationship, you're setting yourself up for disappointment. Compromise is the basis of a good partnership. However, it takes effort on each party's part to ensure that there is a fair exchange.

Recognize your partner's interests.

Knowing what your partner values most will go a long way toward cultivating goodwill and an environment of consensus. On the other hand, it's important that your partner understands your desires and that you express them clearly. Constantly putting every other person's needs ahead of your own can only lead to frustration and rage.

Don't set yourself the objective of "winning."

It will be impossible to find a compromise if you approach your partner with the mentality that things must be done your way or else. This attitude can stem from a lack of needs being met when you were younger, or it may be the result of years of cumulative frustration in the relationship reaching a boiling point. It is ok to be passionate about something, but your partner has a right to be heard as well. Respect the other person and their point of view.

Learn how to handle conflicts in a friendly manner.

Conflict is unavoidable in any relationship, but both parties must feel heard for a relationship to remain strong. The aim is to preserve and deepen the relationship rather than to win.

Make sure you are fighting fair. Keep your mind on the job at hand and show respect for the other person. Don't start a war over something you can't fix.

Don't attack someone directly, However, to express how you feel, use "I" statements. Instead of saying, "You make me feel bad," try saying, "I feel bad when you do that."

Don't drag old arguments into the mix. Rather than assigning blame for past problems or grudges, concentrate on what you can do right now to fix the issue.

Be willing to forgive. If you're reluctant or unable to forgive others, you'll never be able to resolve a dispute.

If tempers flare, take a break. Before you do or say something you'll regret, take a few minutes to relieve tension and calm down. Always bear in mind that you're arguing with someone you care about.

Know when to let something go. Agree to disagree if you can't come to an understanding. An argument needs two people to keep going. You can opt to disengage and move on if a fight isn't going anywhere.

Tip 5: Be ready for ups and downs

Every partnership has its ups and downs, which must be remembered. You won't always agree on anything. Often, one of the partners is coping with a difficult situation, such as a near family member's death. Other incidents, such as job loss or serious health issues, may affect both spouses and find it difficult to relate to one another. You may have different ideas about how to handle your finances or raise your children.

Different people deal with stress in different ways, and miscommunications can easily escalate into frustration and rage.

Do not take out your problems on your partner. Life's pressures will make us irritable. When you're under a lot of tension, it can seem easier to vent to your mate, or even better, to yell at them. Fighting like this may feel good at first, but it will eventually poison your relationship. Other better ways to deal with tension, indignation, and frustration can be found.

Trying to force a solution can cause more problems. Every individual approaches problems and issues in their own unique way. Keep in mind that you're part of a community. Keeping moving forward together will help you get through the difficult times.

Look back to the early stages of your relationship. Discuss the events that brought you together, the point at which you started to break apart, and how you can work together to rekindle the feeling of falling in love.

Be open to change. Change is unavoidable in life, and you can either embrace it or fight it. Flexibility is essential to adjust to the constant change that occurs in every relationship, and it helps you to develop together in both good and bad times.

CHAPTER 9: THE GOLDEN RULES FOR A HAPPY AND LASTING RELATIONSHIP

Pope Francis reminded the United States Congress of the Golden Rule, saying, "Do unto others as you would have them do unto you."

The pope was talking to immigrants and refugees in particular. However, when people marry, they become a miniature society with a social justice system. The way partners conduct business reflects their beliefs about fairness, justice, and sensitivity.

Unfortunately, many partners interpret these ideas based on how they are affected rather than how they interact. We may claim that acting in self-interest rather than empathy is a defect in human nature.

Marriage is a governmental, societal, or religiously recognized interpersonal partnership that is usually intimate and sexual and is frequently formed as a contract or civil process. The legal idea of marriage is a civil marriage.

In the most common type of marriage, a man and a woman become husband and wife. Other types of marriage occur as well; polygamy, in which a person has multiple spouses (marriage partners), is widespread in many cultures.

Legal, social, and economic stability; the construction of a family unit; procreation and the education and caring of children; legitimizing sexual encounters; public confession of love are just a few of the reasons people marry.

Wedding ceremonies may be performed by a religious official, a similar government-sanctioned secular official, or a trusted friend of the wedding partners. Marriage frequently involves duties between the individuals involved, as well as their extended families in many societies. Find a mate

It is vital to select a suitable companion to marry. A person who wishes to marry can find a mate through a-wooing procedure. Alternatively, a third party may match two marriageable people, with the union normally only being formalized if both applicants agree. An arranged marriage is what it's called.

The person seeking marriage or his or her parents decide between courting and planned marriage. Parents may be willing to compel an arranged marriage in some cases due to cultural tradition (e.g., in the Middle East) or other particular circumstances (e.g., dowry). However, it is worth mentioning that in many circumstances, the person seeking marriage is fine with having his or her marriage arranged and would freely choose an arranged marriage regardless of the parental desire. Actual forced marriage occurs in only a few cultures and is frequently met with strong criticism, even from those who support arranged marriages in general.

If given the option, whether a person prefers courtship or planned marriage depends on whether they feel marriage should be founded on feeling or logic. A person on one extreme of the spectrum believes that there is only one "soul mate" who is right for them. During the wooing period of a relationship, a partner is often chosen based on the depth of emotional connection they have with their spouse. A person on the other end of the spectrum believes that there are many appropriate mates and sees marriage primarily as a method of starting a family. The deep emotional tie between spouses that characterizes strong marriages is more likely to be perceived as something that can be formed with an ideal partner via nurture and cultivation. The majority of people fall somewhere in the middle of these two extremes.

Obligations and rights

Marriage quite often establishes the legal father of a woman's child; establishes the legal mother of a man's child; establishes the control of the husband or his family over the wife's sexual services, labor, and property; establishes the control of the wife or her family over the husband's sexual services, labor, and property; establishes the control of the husband or his family over the wife's sexual services, labor, and property; establishes the control None of these privileges are granted to marriage in all societies, and none are universal.

Having children does not need marriage. About 30.1% of births in the United States in 1992 were to unmarried mothers. Sometimes married couples opt not to have children or cannot produce children due to age or infertility. In some societies, women are obligated to bear children when they marry. In northern Ghana, for example, bridewealth payment indicates a woman's obligation to bear children, and women who utilize birth control fear serious physical abuse and retaliation.

The majority of the world's main religions advise couples to marry before having sexual relations. Unmarried persons should not have sex, which they refer to as fornication, according to them. Fornication is sometimes socially frowned upon, if not outright criminalized. Adultery, or having sex with a married person other than one's husband, is widely condemned by all major global faiths and is frequently criminalized. It's also against the US military's guiding law. Nonetheless, three recent studies in the United

States utilizing nationally representative samples revealed that approximately 10-15% of women and 20-25% of men participate in extramarital sex.

Maintaining Relationships

Relationship maintenance refers to the practices that partners engage in to keep a relationship satisfied and extend its lifespan.

Open marriage has a variety of effects on relationships, including positive, neutral, and bad consequences. Some couples enjoy long-term open marriages and claim high levels of marital satisfaction. Other couples abandon their open marriages and revert to sexual monogamy. Other couples have major issues and claim that their open marriage contributed to their divorce.

Scientists are still perplexed as to why some couples respond favorably to open marriage while others do not. They also have no way of knowing whether couples will respond positively or adversely. As a result, all open-marriage couples may want to pay attention to their relationship maintenance habits.

The subject of relationship maintenance activities is just too extensive for a single book to handle. Here are a few instances of relationship maintenance strategies. Other than the ones described here, readers should be aware that there are several ways to maintain healthy and happy partnerships.

Six fundamental guidelines for resolving conflicts and maintaining healthy marriages:

o When a conflict escalates, we will call a Time Out or Stop Action and either

(a) try again using the Speaker-Listener technique or

(b) agree to talk about the issue later, at a specific time, using the Speaker-Listener strategy.

o We'll employ the Speaker-Listener approach when we're having problems communicating.

o When employing the Speaker-Listener methodology, we shall keep problem discussion and problem solution separate (i.e., we will discuss the nature of the problem before jumping too quickly to finding solutions).

o We can bring up difficulties at any time, but a partner has the right to say, "This is not the right time." If a partner refuses to speak at that time, he or she is responsible for arranging a time to speak shortly.

o We'll have "couple's meetings" once a week.

o We'll set aside time for the important things in life, such as enjoyment, companionship, and sensuality. We'll agree to keep these periods free of conflict and the need to resolve problems.

You've probably learned what relationship norms exist and are doing your best to follow them if you've made your fair share of blunders in past relationships. But it's not going to happen. Most of these pieces of advice are out of date and don't apply to all situations, so it's best to toss them to the curb.

1. Wait for him to initiate the conversation.

Whether it's in bed or in any other aspect of your relationship, the best rule to follow is that if you feel like doing something, don't allow anything stops you. Don't expect him to finish everything first every time.

2. Be best friends with each other.

While best friends are the first people you turn to for support when you need it, they don't f*ck with one other. Stick to being his girlfriend solely unless you're okay with not being able to sext and have sex with your guy.

3. Be completely honest with each other.

For the sake of honesty, telling your lover that he's a poor kisser or that you despise his wardrobe choices won't help your relationship last. So, if you want to spend as much time with him as possible, keep in mind that no-holds-barred honesty should only apply to you and your pet.

4. Never go to bed angry.

Staying up late to work out your problems with your lover when you know you're not in the best of moods isn't a wise or mature decision. Instead, go to bed and sleep on it, so you and your lover don't have to deal with any extra stress or sleep deprivation. After a good night's sleep, you'll be astonished at how much wiser you'll act.

5. Fight.

Even the longest and most stable relationships have their share of petty and major disputes. That isn't to say you should quarrel with your lover over every issue where your viewpoints differ. Fights can be taxing and taxing, and they aren't always as healthy as people believe. More significantly, there are considerably more effective and wiser solutions to your problems.

6. Give ultimatums when necessary.

Don't be tricked into thinking that asking your significant other to choose between you and his mother, pal, puppy, or other things you believe are more important to him than you is the correct thing to do. Doing so will force him to do something he doesn't want to do, and he may dislike you as a result. Is that the kind of circumstance you'd like to be in?

7. Make it difficult to achieve what you want.

Your boyfriend's brain is designed to enjoy the thrill of the chase, but he's told you before that dealing with you while you're playing your hard-to-get card isn't always pleasurable. This does not imply that you should make everything simple for him to obtain. He'll still have to work for a while but be there for him when he needs you.

8. Sex should never be scheduled.

Because you should have sex with your guy whenever and wherever you want because of YOLO, this concept is extremely appealing, but it quickly becomes too hot to bear as life unfolds. So, before you succumb to life's inevitable sense of timing, set aside some time for some much-needed pillow chat and hugging.

CONCLUSION

The question remains: for the sake of growth, can you tolerate discomfort? It will stir your fear to create a strong self. But you reinforce your emotional muscles each time you abstain from reassurance seeking and regulating behaviors. Will you be able to keep a line with yourself? Will you self-confront and readjust when you start to over-depend on your partner?

Use your relationship anxiety as an opportunity to learn how to transfer your pain into personal development. What if this wound of abandonment is an invitation to reorganize yourself into a resilient individual? It is only when we measure our potential that the power that exists in us can be discovered.

Printed in Great Britain
by Amazon